MW01283040

5th and Main, Paris, Ky., 1909. [Photo from the collection of Tom Moore]

IN THE COURTHOUSE'S SHADOW

The Lynching of George Carter in Paris, Kentucky

Tessa Bishop Hoggard

Murky Press

Copyright © 2021 by Tessa Bishop Hoggard
All rights reserved.
ISBN: 978-0-9992540-4-2

Murky Press
www.murkypress.com
Book design: Sallie Showalter

ENSLAVED

by Claude McKay
1889–1948

Oh when I think of my long-suffering race,
For weary centuries despised, oppressed,
Enslaved and lynched, denied a human place
In the great life line of the Christian West;
And in the Black Land disinherited,
Robbed in the ancient country of its birth,
My heart grows sick with hate, becomes as lead,
For this my race that has no home on earth.
Then from the dark depths of my soul I cry
To the avenging angel to consume
The white man's world of wonders utterly:
Let it be swallowed up in earth's vast womb,
Or upward roll as sacrificial smoke
To liberate my people from its yoke!

This book is dedicated to the memory of my mother, Lorine Bishop (1931–2020), a collector of many things, especially antiques, books, art, and black history.

I also dedicate this story to Lindrell Blackwell, a friend and partner in ancestry research, who encouraged me to write this story about the 1901 lynching in Bourbon County, Ky. In the photo, he kneels on the Carter family plot in Cedar Heights Cemetery, Paris, Ky.

CONTENTS

This gate, currently adjacent to the historic Duncan Tavern in Paris, Ky., marked the entrance to the Bourbon County Courthouse in 1901. The original eagle, which had been damaged over time, has been replaced by one created by artist and Paris native Adalin Wichman.

PREFACE

For over a century, secrets shrouded in hushed rumors echoed through Bourbon County, Ky. Disrobing those secrets can be painful, yet necessary for healing to occur.

Presiding over one of those secrets is a large iron eagle that proudly spreads its wings above a wrought-iron gate. A steel rod supports the eagle above the arch. Between 1872 and 1901, the gate—said to be imported from Wales—welcomed visitors to the Bourbon County Courthouse.

But, in February 1901, an angry mob used that supporting rod to lynch a 21-year-old black man accused of assaulting a white woman. The eagle was a silent witness to the atrocity. Eight months later, the courthouse was destroyed by fire, and only the wrought-iron gate with its sharp-eyed eagle was salvaged. Today the gate stands adjacent to the town's historic Duncan Tavern, a quiet testament to that dark moment in the town's history.

Let us gather ourselves upon the eagle's wings and reach back to a time when "Judge Lynch" reigned. Peering through the eagle's eye, let's trace the events preceding the lynching, the day of the lynching, and the aftermath.

Now is the time to loosen the grip of decades of whispered secrets and move forward with a renewed conviction for equal justice for all. For how can a people freely move forward when an injustice shackles us to the past?

Two Families

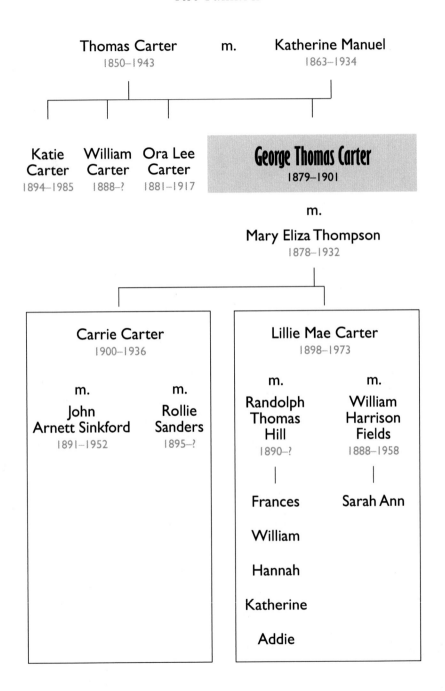

Thomas Carter
1850–1943

m.

Katherine Manuel
1863–1934

Katie Carter
1894–1985

William Carter
1888–?

Ora Lee Carter
1881–1917

George Thomas Carter
1879–1901

m.

Mary Eliza Thompson
1878–1932

Carrie Carter
1900–1936

m.
John Arnett Sinkford
1891–1952

m.
Rollie Sanders
1895–?

Lillie Mae Carter
1898–1973

m.
Randolph Thomas Hill
1890–?

Frances

William

Hannah

Katherine

Addie

m.
William Harrison Fields
1888–1958

Sarah Ann

Paris, Ky.

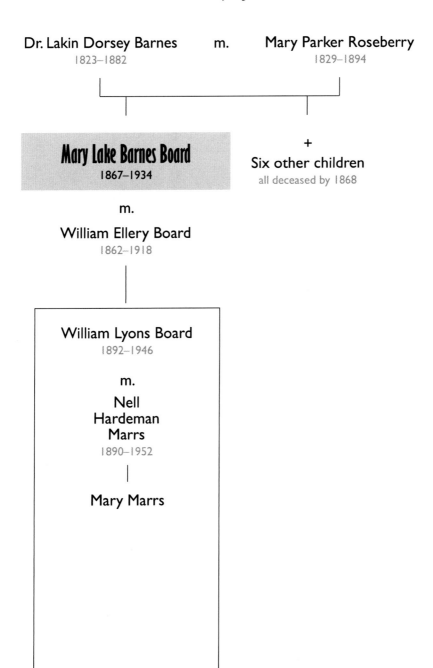

Dr. Lakin Dorsey Barnes   m.   Mary Parker Roseberry
1823–1882   1829–1894

Mary Lake Barnes Board
1867–1934

+
Six other children
all deceased by 1868

m.
William Ellery Board
1862–1918

William Lyons Board
1892–1946

m.
Nell
Hardeman
Marrs
1890–1952

Mary Marrs

INTRODUCTION

In an interview conducted in 1988 by staff at the University of Kentucky, my grandfather C. Maceo Bishop recalled, "People were scared during those days because they were looking for a negro."[1] *Those days* were when white mobs took matters into their own hands and terrorized the black community. Lynch law was mob violence intended to enforce racial subordination and segregation.

According to historian George C. Wright, "The first decade after slavery is significant for a complete understanding of racial violence in the Bluegrass State. Lynchings did not start all at once in the late 1880s but had been a part of white oppression of Afro-Americans since the beginning of emancipation."[2] Though the exact number will never be known, Wright estimates that at least 353 people in Kentucky died at the hands of lynch mobs between the end of the Civil War and 1940. Furthermore, he states that "Of this number, 258 or 73 percent were Afro-Americans." It's important to note that his estimate does not include people who simply "disappeared" after being in the hands of law officers and the ones whose lives were spared by the mob on the promise that the state would quickly execute them.[3]

William O'Connell Bradley (1847–1914), the first Republican Governor of Kentucky.

Those wanting to end racism in Kentucky were in the minority but included the state's first Republican governor, William O. Bradley [1895–1899]. He was elected with strong support from African Americans and called a special legislative session in March 1897 to consider an antilynching bill. Both houses of the General Assembly passed it, and Gov. Bradley signed it on May 11, 1897.[4]

Though lynchings declined after the bill was passed, they continued to have a stronghold in Kentucky, primarily due to lack of enforcement of the law. One of those lynchings took the life of George Thomas Carter in Bourbon County four years after the bill was signed.

Bourbon County was one of nine counties organized by the Virginia Legislature before Kentucky became a state. Its county seat is Paris, which was chartered in 1789 under the name of Hopewell, Va. The name was changed to Paris the following year in appreciation of French aid during the American Revolution.

Main Street at the 500 block, Paris, Ky., circa 1898, when the population was about 4,600. [Historic Paris photos courtesy of the Hopewell Museum and The Citizen Advertiser]

Authors Karl Raitz and Nancy O'Malley describe Paris' geography: "The meandering Houston and Stoner creeks, two major tributaries of the Licking River's South Fork, join here in a way that created a broad-shouldered peninsula flanked by streams on three sides."[5] Paris has a total area of 6.0 square miles and is located 18 miles northeast of Lexington, Ky. Its population as of 2018 was 9,872.

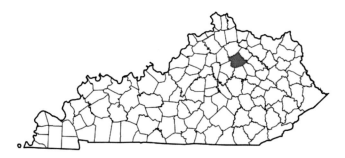

Map of Kentucky highlighting Bourbon County. [David Benbennick, Wikimedia Commons]

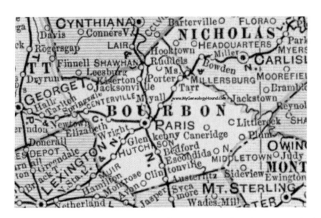

Map of Bourbon County, 1905. [Cram's Ideal Reference Atlas]

Maceo Bishop was born in 1898 and raised in Paris, Ky. He was 2 years old when George Carter was lynched, but he heard accounts of the event from his parents and other senior family members. After a black man allegedly assaulted a white woman, Mrs. W. E. Board, on the brisk night of December 3, 1900, the hunt was on for someone to pay for the crime.

The local newspapers reported rumors of imminent mob justice and pronounced the man's sentence before a suspect had even been identified.

"They just wanted a negro to hang during those times," continued Bishop.[6] Even though evidence or absence thereof might have suggested that the accused was innocent, the mob's thirst for blood—any black man's blood—prevailed.

In that era, the arms of justice typically failed to embrace African Americans. Even black defendants afforded trials were "tried in hostile environments with judges and juries convinced of their guilt before hearing any evidence."[7] Blacks dared not speak openly or challenge the accusers for fear of suffering repercussions; they instead spoke amongst themselves in fearful whispers. "Given the reality of white violence and the oppressive white legal system that punished them for the smallest offense, most Kentucky blacks well knew the risk of resorting to violence to protest racial discrimination," explains Wright.[8] Despite the inherent risks, some blacks strongly resisted and denounced lynchings by carrying guns, starting fires, and threatening the lives of known mob leaders.[9]

The trail of atrocities committed by white mobs, the individuals sometimes disguised under masks or white sheets, terrorized and intimidated the black community. Mob justice had no boundaries, and "government officials frequently turned a blind eye or condoned the mob violence."[10]

The Interior Journal of Stanford, Ky., wrote about another Bourbon County lynching in 1889: "The lynching was conducted in a most quiet and orderly manner, showing that the best citizens and not hoodlums, who thirst for human blood, had performed the righteous work."[11] This statement typified the mindset of many lynch mobs. Sadly, twelve years later, in 1901, nothing had changed.

Chapter 1

THE ACCUSED

G eorge Thomas Carter was the firstborn of Thomas "Tom" and Katherine "Kate" Manuel Carter. The 1870 Bourbon County census lists 14-year-old Tom living with his father, Thomas Sr., 8-year-old brother, Isaac, and members of the Henry family.

The Indianapolis News, March 20, 1950, George's Uncle Isaac (Tom Carter's brother)

Funeral Arranged for Isaac Carter

Isaac E. Carter, 85, former Claypool Hotel waiter, will be buried in Crown Hill Cemetery following services at 2:30 p.m. tomorrow in Bethel AME Church.

He died Saturday in his home, 714 Fayette St. Born at Lawrenceburg, Ky., Mr. Carter had lived in Indianapolis 60 years. A waiter 52 years, he had started at the old Bates House, working there after it became the Claypool, until his retirement eight years ago. He was a member of Bethel AME Church.

Survivors are four daughters, the Misses Cora and Deradetta Carter, Mrs. Flora Bates and Mrs. Alice Bowins; three sons, Isaac Carter, Jr., and Perry and Paul Carter, six grandchildren and two great-grandchildren.

Tom's 12-year-old brother, Levi, lived separately and worked as a domestic servant in the Donley household. Though George was born in Paris, Ky., his paternal family appears to have migrated to Paris from Lawrenceburg, Ky., based on his Uncle Isaac's obituary.

According to the 1870 Bourbon County census, George's mother, Kate, was an 11-year-old residing with her parents, William and Emily Manuel, and her younger siblings, William, Grant, and Narcissa. Her father, William Manuel, was a carpenter. The Manuels came to Bourbon County from nearby Clark County, Ky., where Kate was born.

| 1870 United States Federal Census for Kate Mannel | | | | | | | | |
| Kentucky › Bourbon › Paris | | | | | | | | |
Dwelli No.	Family No.	Name	Age	Sex	Race	Occupation	Real Estate	Personal Estate
132	170	Mannel Willie	40	M	B	Carpenter		
		— Emily	35	F	B	Keeping house		
		— Kate	11	F	BB	at Home		
		— William	7	M	B			
		— Grant	4	M	B			
		Mannel Narcissa	1	F	B			

* Person on last line is 1-yr old Narcissa Manuel (copied from next page of census)

George's parents—Tom and Kate—had been born into slavery, the property of white men. Both were under the age of 10 when President Abraham Lincoln issued the Emancipation Proclamation. Although the Proclamation was to take effect January 1, 1863, slavery did not legally end in the U.S. until December 18, 1865. At that time, Kentucky began to gradually emancipate its slaves.

Following a life of bondage, freedmen experienced both sweet freedom and intensified oppression. For many white people, being on equal grounds with blacks was inconceivable. According to historian H. E. Everman, the freedman was transformed from a piece of property to a person with social and political rights.[1] Resentment of the freedman manifested in violent acts of white supremacy and intimidation through racial terrorism.

Records at the Hopewell Museum in Paris indicate that nearly 7,000 slaves were emancipated in Bourbon County. "After the Civil War, the newly freed citizens of Bourbon County overwhelmingly moved away from the farms on which they had been enslaved to exclusively black communities while they still worked for whites, often the former owners."[2] The freedmen faced social and economic dilemmas: little or no money and little or no education. Former slave Houston Hartsfield Holloway wrote: "…we colored people did not know how to be free and the white people did not know how to have a free colored person about them."[3]

In 1865 the Freedmen's Bureau was established to help former slaves and poor whites in the South with food, housing, medical aid, and legal assistance. However, it failed to safeguard blacks from exploitation and abuse.

During the late 1870s Tom and Kate married and made their home in Bourbon County. Marriage was one of those privileges appreciated by freedmen; even when a slave owner had permitted it, marriage between slaves was not considered valid or legal.

Tom and Kate soon started their family. George was born in July 1879—the first family member not born into slavery. George was legally theirs to love and protect; he was not the property of a slave owner. He could not be separated from them or sold down river. As with most parents, the Carters' hope was that their offspring would have a better life than they did, including educational and employment opportunities.

By the 1880 census, 1-year-old George and his parents were boarders in the Cage household in Ruckerville, one of two black communities in the town of Paris. Ruckerville was in the northern section of town on Houston Creek along 2nd Street, also known as Peacock Road. Tom was a laborer and Kate a "wash woman" or laundress. In the 1900 census, Tom is listed as a farm laborer and Kate a cook.

During this era, the majority of African American women were employed as field workers, house servants, waitresses, and laundresses. Black men in Bourbon County typically worked on farms where owners grew hemp and tobacco, both labor-intensive crops. The jobs were usually low-paying, very demanding, and often demeaning. My grandfather Maceo Bishop said that it was rough during those times. Blacks worked whatever job they could find to take care of their families.

As a free man, Tom did quite well in a racist environment. Though illiterate, he completed his first real estate transaction only 21 years after emancipation. On September 1, 1884, he purchased Lot No. 10 on Brooks Street in Ruckerville from Henry and Nancy Nichols for $140. In September 1892, he purchased a second property, Lot No. 11, from W. T. and Helen Brooks for $130, which he paid in two installments over a 12-month period.

Those acquisitions were significant, as an exhibit at the Hopewell Museum explained: "Each time a freed slave managed to buy a house and lot, the transaction symbolized a long-sought right that whites took for granted but people of color did not."[4]

250 Brooks Street, Paris, Ky.: Childhood home of George T. Carter, built by his father, Tom. [Image captured June 2012]

Tom was a responsible and disciplined man who built houses on his two lots for less than $800 each. Since his father-in-law was a carpenter, Tom most likely benefited from his expert assistance. His primary homestead consisted of four large rooms, front and back porches, a cellar/basement used to store coal and canned goods, a well outside for water, a two-seater outhouse, an outside storage facility, and a chicken house. Tom's efficient home design reveals "a man ahead of himself." The house is no longer owned by the Carter family but still stands today after more than a century, a credit to Tom's skillful craftsmanship.

Seven children were born to Tom and Kate, but only four survived as of the 1900 census. George was a proud big brother to Ora Lee, William (Willie), and Katie.

Both Tom and Kate understood the importance of educating their four children. This privilege escaped them as enslaved people. Though Kentucky law permitted slaves to learn to read and write, this, too, was contingent upon the slave owner's approval. The Freedmen's Bureau made some strides by establishing schools for black children, but "the quality of education received by black students at these institutions was extremely poor, and the reasons were obvious: the schools had virtually no financial resources, lacked trained teachers, and their physical plants were totally inadequate."[5]

Despite these challenges, Tom and Kate ensured that their children had access to the best education available to them. As shown in the Bourbon County KY Colored 1897 School Census, three of the four Carter children were enrolled in school that year. According to a Bourbon News' article dated 1898, "The colored school has a well-arranged seven-room building. The average enrollment is 350."[6] Paris Western High School, which George and Ora Lee most likely attended, was one of the state's only colored high schools in the 1890s, according to H. E. Everman,.[7] The youngest child, Katie, was 3 years old in 1897, too young to start school.

Bourbon County KY Colored 1897 School Census
Paris District

Excerpt:

Parent/Guardian	Child	Sex	Age
Carter, Tom	Geo	M	17
	Ora Lee	F	15
	Will	M	11

Source: Kentucky African American Griots [http://sites.rootsweb.com]

At the age of 19, George became a father. His daughter Lillie Mae was born in July 1898. A few months later he married Lillie Mae's mother, Mary Eliza Thompson.

```
        Partial Listing of the Marriage Register of Colored Persons
                          In Bourbon Co. KY.
                             1835 - 1933
                Transcribed and submitted by C. Harvey


    EXCERPT:


    1898
    July 27           James Jackson              Priscilla Simpson
    Jan. 5            Berry Riddell              Molina Bradley
    Sept 26           Samuel Wells               Maggie  Molden
    Sept. 26          Hayden Fields              Annie Goodman
    Sept. 29          William Burns              Mary Lannen
    Sept. 29          Allen Thomas               Susie Weekly
    Oct. 12           James B. Moberly           Alice Marshall
    Oct 19            Charles Berry              Maggie Deavers
    Oct. 19           George T. Carter           Mary E. Thompson
    Oct. 29           James Latham               Marcella Hauffman
```

Source: Kentucky African American Griots [http://sites.rootsweb.com]

As with many newlyweds, their first year of marriage was filled with adjustments. George's biggest challenge was the financial responsibility of supporting a family when good job opportunities for African Americans were scarce. George also faced legal issues seven months after he and Mary Eliza married. He had an altercation with William "Bud" Williams and was subsequently arrested. He was charged with the crime of malicious cutting and wounding with intent to kill. The $100 bail was not paid, and George was subsequently committed to jail. He waived his right to an examining trial and was held over for trial during the June term of the Bourbon Circuit Court.

A handwritten transcript of the jury instructions read:

> *"If the jury believe from the evidence that the defendant at the time he cut the said Williams if he did cut him, he believed and had reasonable grounds to believe that the said Williams was thru and thru about to take his life or inflict on him great bodily harm and there appeared to him in the exercise of a reasonable judgment no other safe means to avert its then real or to him apparent danger if any but to cut the said Williams then he had the right so to do and they ought to acquit him on the grounds of self defense."[8]*

What precipitated the altercation is unknown, but based on the foregoing instructions to the jury, George pled not guilty due to self-defense. Nevertheless, the jury found him guilty and sentenced him to confinement and hard labor in the state penitentiary for the term of one year and six months.

George must have been released early, however, because the 1900 Census (shown on page 12), compiled less than a year later, reports that George and his wife and 2-year old daughter, Lillie Mae, are living in Ruckerville in the household of his mother-in-law, Mary (Mollie) Thompson, a widow. The Thompson household was a full one. Other household members included Mary Thompson's two sons, five daughters, and another son-in-law, Will Smoot (husband of Bessie). George worked as a day laborer to support his family.

Carter's second daughter, Carrie, was born a few weeks after the 1900 census was completed.

In this relatively calm period of his young life, George, juggled his roles as the son of Tom and Kate Carter, brother to Ora Lee, Willie, and Katie, husband to Mary Eliza, and father to Lillie Mae and Carrie.

1900 census for the Thompson household, which included George and Mary
Carter with 2-year-old daughter, Lillie. Note that errors by census takers were
common. For example, the age of George's daughter, misspelled Lilly,
is incorrectly listed as 11. She turned 2 the next month.

Chapter 2

THE ACCUSER

Mary Lake Barnes was born in Paris, Ky., on June 2, 1867, the youngest child of Dr. Lakin D. and Mary P. Roseberry Barnes. Lake's father was one of the pioneer physicians of Paris. Their family home on High Street adjacent to the Episcopal Church no longer stands, but it was once a local landmark.

The Bourbon News, Paris, Ky., Friday, July 2, 1920

H. L. Mitchell & Son, real estate agents, sold recently for Mrs. Ruby L. Arnsparger the old Barnes property, located on High street, adjoining the Episcopal church, to Cash Crow, for $2,000. The property has been leased to Mr. Hall, employed by the A. F. Wheeler Furniture Co. This is one of the landmarks of Paris. It was the home in the early days of Paris of Dr. L. D. Barnes, prominent physician, father of Mrs. Wm. E. Board, now residing in Louisville.

Grief was a frequent visitor in the Barnes household. Six of the seven children of Dr. and Mrs. L. D. Barnes predeceased them. By July 1868, when Lake was only 1 year old, she was the sole surviving child. She nonetheless thrived in a highly respected household headed by a man of strict morals and conservative principles. Dr. Barnes provided financially for his family, which included servants, and promoted his daughter's education.

Mary Lake Barnes

Lake attended Daughters College in Harrodsburg, Ky., in the 1880s, which was then under the direction of Mr. John Augustus Williams, the founder of Christian College in Columbia, S.C., who had also been the president of Bacon College in Harrodsburg. Mr. Williams was born in Bourbon County in 1824. In 1917, Daughters College was sold and eventually converted into Beaumont Inn. Embracing its past, the inn's recorded history explains Mr. Williams' devotion to his students: "Having lost his only two daughters in their early teens, Williams took the students under his arm of fatherhood and said, 'all of these girls will be my daughters' and he guided their education as if they had been his own."[1]

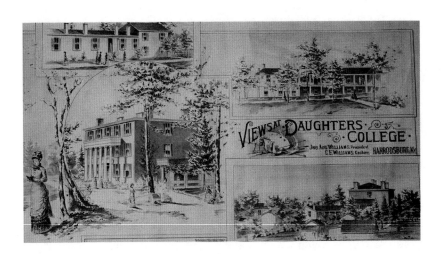

SIR KNIGHT
WILLIAM E. BOARD,
EMINENT GRAND WARDER

Many suitors vied for the hand of Mary Lake Barnes, but only one won her heart, William (Bill) Ellery Board, a native of Harrodsburg. Bill was described as a man of pleasing address and genial manners who attracted friends readily. He was highly thought of by his associates in business and fraternal organizations, and, as "Billy" Board, was welcomed to all circles.[2]

Bill had transferred with the Adams Express Company from Danville, Ky., to Paris in 1886. The company was a freight and cargo transport business that had its beginnings in the early 1800s. Bill took charge of the Baltimore & Ohio company's business at Paris. "His departure was regretted by Danville's businessmen and citizens. He won for himself many friends here by his prompt attention and uniform politeness."[3]

Kentucky Advocate, Danville, Ky.,
December 9, 1887

THE marriage of Mr. W. E. Board, of this place, and Miss Lake Barnes, of Paris, is announced to take place the 12th of January, at the Christian church, Paris, Rev. J. S. Sweeney officiating. Billie is Adams Express agent at Paris and a modest young man. The wedding will be one to the toniest ever held in the capital of Bourbon, there being twelve bridesmaids and twenty-four attendants, including ushers. Some of the groomsmen will be selected from Harrodsburg and Danville. Here is to you, Billie, hoping your shadow may never grow less and all your troubles be little ones. Miss Barnes is a former pupil of Daughters College.

Shortly after Bill transferred to Paris, he and Lake married at the Paris Christian Church. The Kentucky Advocate records the details of the elaborate wedding. After the ceremony, a reception was held at the residence of Lake's mother. Then the bridal pair left by train for the East.

Less than a month after the wedding, Bill's joy turned to sorrow when his beloved father, Richard Board Sr., died. His father had been the Circuit Clerk in Mercer County, Ky., for twenty-four consecutive years.

By the 1900 census, Lake Board had birthed three children but only one was still living, William Lyons Board. The family boarded in the household of Lavinia Wilmoth on 2nd Street. Yet another full house included Mrs. Wilmoth's daughter, son-in-law, and three sons.

Bill eventually accepted a position as bookkeeper with the Deposit Bank of Paris. He continued in the capacity of bookkeeper for several years until he entered the insurance field.

1905   *2019 [Google]*

"Since its organization in 1851 it [Deposit Bank of Paris] has responded with fidelity to needs of the community in money matters, earning for itself a record which invites and fosters confidence."[4] The bank was inactivated in 1984 due to a merger, but the building is still in use. Location is 400 Main Street, Paris, Ky. [Paris historic photos courtesy of the Hopewell Museum and The Citizen Advertiser]

Outside of his employment, Bill was an active member of the fraternal club Knights Templar and held various leadership positions, including Eminent Commander. He traveled extensively throughout Kentucky as a delegate representing his lodge and frequently participated in meetings and elaborate banquets. Sir Knight W. E. Board and his fair lady were hosts to grand receptions in their home.

Bill was also a member of the Paris bowling team. He was a competitive bowler and was often the highest scorer at the local bowling lane.

The Bourbon News, Paris, Ky., Friday,
November 11, 1898

Bits About Bowlers.

A bowling league has been organized in Louisville. Why not organize one in Paris? There are enough good players in Paris to form half a dozen clubs.

Walter Davis scored 219 last night at the Pastime Alleys.

W. E. Board is the latest player to enter the 200 list. He scored 204 Tuesday night in the match game with the Paris team.

The Paris team which defeated Mt. Sterling was defeated Tuesday night by a picked team of Paris players. The picked team won three out of four games.

The Paris team will go to Mt. Sterling to-night to play a series of games with the Mt. Sterling team. It is expected that quite a delegation will go with the boys. Mt. Sterling people are offering prizes to the player making the best score.

The Bourbon News, Paris, Ky., Friday,
October 5, 1900

Secret Order News.

THE Masonic Lodge will to-night have three Grand officers as their guests— Grand Master John M. Ramsey, of Owingsville, Grand Senior Warden Harry Bailey, of Cynthiana, and Grand Junior Warden John W. Landram, of Mayfield—at the lodge meeting. The third degree will be conferred upon George R. Davis and W. E. Board. After the ceremonies a banquet will be served at the Windsor Hotel. The following will be the menu:

CELERY.   PICKLES.   OLIVES.

COLD SLICED HAM.   COLD TONGUE.

CRANBERRY SAUCE.

CLARET PUNCH.

CHICKEN SALAD.   POTATO SALAD.

SLICED TOMATOES.

ASPARAGUS TIPS.   PEAS.

ICE CREAM.   ASSORTED CAKE.

COFFEE.

CREAM CHEESE.   WAFERS.

FRUIT.

WINE.   CIGARS.

Lake's social calendar was also busy, including membership in the Jemima Johnson Chapter of the D. A. R. (Daughters of the American Revolution), for which she served as Regent.

MRS. MARY LAKE BARNES BOARD.   16134
        Born in Paris, Bourbon County, Kentucky.
Wife of William E. Board.
Descendant of Lieut. John Barnes.
Daughter of Dr. Lakin Dorsey Barnes (b. 1823) and Mary Parker Roseberry, his wife.
Granddaughter of Joseph Barnes and Phoebe Stockton (b. 1782), his wife (m. 1800).
Gr.-granddaughter of John Barnes.
John Barnes entered the army as a private, 1776. He rose to the rank of lieutenant in the Virginia Continental Line and was retired, 1781. He was born in England and died in Jefferson Co., Va.

The Daughters of the American Revolution is a lineage-based membership service organization for women who are directly descended from a person involved in the United States' efforts towards independence. [Source: Lineage Book by the Daughters of the American Revolution, Volume XVII]

In 1901, Mary Lake Board was a 32-year-old wife and mother when George Carter was lynched in Paris, Ky.

Chapter 3

1900-01 NEWSPAPER SOURCES

I have primarily used newspaper articles from 1900 and 1901 to reconstruct the lynching incident, but it's important to note the potential for editorial bias in that era. For example, newspapers commonly promoted ethnic and racial stereotypes by reporting all negro crimes and misbehavior. "Negro drinking, fighting, gambling, and shootings seemed typical in rural areas, in Paris, and at fairs and festivals."[1] Derogatory drawings and stories painted alleged African American criminals in an intentionally unflattering light. As George C. Wright states, "Indeed, even before standing trial, blacks were found guilty in the white press, denounced in very harsh and derogatory terms."[2]

Unfortunately, even today biased reporting is a serious concern that contradicts our democratic principles. In 2020 James Wright described such reporting as "myopic journalism."[3] He further states that, "Biased, uncritical, and narrow framing corners us, compelling us to be complicit in the sanitizing of vigilante violence that continues to harm Black and Indigenous people and communities of color, as well as threatens the health and well-being of all communities."[4]

In the case of George Carter's hanging, newspapers across America reported details of that lawless night in 1901, many perhaps purposefully distorting the facts. Some accounts exaggerated the incident or fabricated details to incite an angry nation and to justify the mob's actions.

W. Swift Champ, editor/owner of
The Bourbon News. [Photo from
The Bourbon News, October 3, 1905]

Bruce Miller, editor/owner of
The Kentuckian-Citizen. [Photo
courtesy of the Hopewell Museum]

Paris' local newspapers, The Kentuckian-Citizen and The Bourbon News, contained information not found in other papers, but their biased reporting was undeniable. At the time of the lynching, Lake Board's cousin, Bruce Miller, owned The Kentuckian-Citizen. W. Swift Champ, a dear friend of the Board family, owned The Bourbon News. These associations may have guaranteed favorable treatment of the Boards in their publications.

Excerpt from The Bourbon News, Paris, Ky.,
June 8, 1900

—Mr. and Mrs. Swift Champ enter-
tained a few friends at euchre Wednes-
day evening at their home on Pleasant
street. The players were Mr. and Mrs.
E. M. Dickson, Mr. and Mrs. Thompson,
Tarr, Mr. and Mrs. John T. Ireland,
Mr. and Mrs. T. E. Moore, Jr., Mr. and
Mrs. George Stuart, Mr. and Mrs. W. E.
Board, Mr. and Mrs. Frank P. Clay, Jr.,
Mr. and Mrs. Bruce Miller, Mr. and

W. Swift Champ and Bruce Miller, local news-
paper editors/owners, traveled in the same social
circle as the Board family.

Based on the details reported by the local papers, it also seems clear that reporters were either eyewitnesses, participants, or close associates of the lynching mob.

As we review the events preceding, during, and after the lynching, we must be cognizant of the racial overtones that characterized news reporting during that era in America's history.

Chapter 4

A CLIMATE OF OPPRESSION

I t was not only an era of biased reporting, but also of segregationist Jim Crow laws requiring separate facilities for whites and blacks on public transportation and in schools, hospitals, and restaurants. In nearly every aspect of their lives, blacks felt the weight of this oppression. In particular, whites seemed determined to prevent blacks from voting. Only a few months before the February 1901 lynching, the Lexington, Ky., Morning Herald reported a "Conspiracy to Oppress and Injure the Negroes" in nearby Paris, Ky.

According to the article, in November 1900 J. B. Hutchcraft (probably R. B. Hutchcraft, a well-known Paris businessman and, interestingly, a regular business partner of W. E. Board) swore out warrants against Albert S. Thompson, a white farmer of Bourbon County, and Samuel Adams and Lee Leary, two black men, for conspiring to injure and oppress negroes. Hutchcraft charged that white Democrats hired blacks to set up games of craps, furnished them the money to play, and had them inveigle other negroes into the game. All the participants were then arrested. Over 60 blacks had been arrested in prior months, and more warrants had been sworn out.

The goal of the conspiracy was to prevent black men from voting in the upcoming elections, scheduled for November 6. "They were tried and given fines and a workout or jail sentence sufficient to keep them confined till after November 6," according to the report.[1] The case was carried before the Federal Court, but the grand jury refused to return an indictment.

The Morning Herald, Lexington, Ky., November 2, 1900

CONSPIRACY TO OPPRESS AND INJURE THE NEGROES

The Charge Against Bourbon Men Brought Before Commissioner Hill; Trick Crap Games Alleged.

Yesterday afternoon Deputy U. S. Marshal Con McCarty brought to Lexington Albert S. Thompson, a white farmer of Bourbon county, and Samuel Adams and Lee Leary, two colored men, whom he arrested in Bourbon county yesterday. The arrests were made on warrants sworn out by J. B. Hutcheraft, of Paris, charging a conspiracy to injure and oppress negroes, under section 5508 of the revised statutes of the United States. All three of those arrested gave bond in the sum of $1,000 to appear before United States Commissioner Hill this morning at 10 o'clock.

On Mr. Thompson's bond, Mr. J. Hal Woodford and Mr. B. M. Renick were sureties, coming to Lexington for the purpose of becoming such. They also brought a power of attorney authorizing them to sign the names of several other leading citizens of Bourbon county, among others, Samuel Bedford, G. C. Thompson and John T. Hinton.

Upon the bonds of the negroes, Mr. Thompson, Mr. Woodford and Mr. Renick were the sureties.

The arrests of the men grew out of a series of warrants which have been sworn out in Bourbon county against a number of negroes for playing craps. The charge is made that the arrests of the negroes on this charge has been for the purpose of preventing them from voting on November 6. They were tried and given fines and a workout or jail sentence sufficient to keep them confined till after November 6. It is charged that not only are warrants sworn out for offenses committed many months since, but that some Democrats in Bourbon have hired negroes to put up games of craps, furnished them the money to play on, and had them inveigle other negroes into the game. The whole lot would then be arrested, the negroes hired testify against those they had gotten to play with them, and a sentence sufficient to keep them from the polls given. It is reported that over sixty negroes have already been arrested and more warrants have been sworn out.

The Evening Bulletin, Maysville, Ky., January 16, 1901

SHORTLY before the November election it will be remembered that Albert S. Thomson, of Bourbon County, was arrested on a charge of intimidating negro voters. Negro crap shooters had been making night hideous near his home and he had them arrested, and this was the basis of his arrest, the Republicans, however, claiming it was simply a conspiracy of Thompson and other Democrats to keep the negroes from voting. The case was carried before the Federal Court and the grand jury has refused to return an indictment. The case was characteristic of the despicable tactics resorted to by Republicans during the last campaign.

Hickman Courier, Hickman, Ky.,
March 2, 1900

THE NEGROES CONTROL.

[From Cadiz Telephone.]

Perhaps it may appear strange, but is nevertheless true, that Kentucky with all her boastfulness of superior cultivation and refinement, is the only State in the Union that is under complete control of the negroes. The negro vote of Kentucky comprise about two thirds of the Republican strength, and there is not a Republican official in the State who was not elected by negro votes. This is a rather bold assertion, but a moment's reflection will satisfy you of its truth.

In many states, including Kentucky, white citizens schemed to reduce voting among black men through either fraud or violence. Whites realized that the right to vote was a powerful tool in the hands of freedmen, and that fear led to attempts to suppress this privilege.

Following slavery, freedmen were ardent supporters of the Republican party, sometimes referred to as the Party of Lincoln, which passed legislation protecting the rights of African Americans. On the other hand, "The Democratic party consistently championed itself as the 'white man's party,' uninterested in the concerns of blacks."[2] George C. Wright explains that Democrats were sometimes victorious in close campaigns by convincing voters of impending doom if the Republicans won.[3] Though many black voters shifted their support to the Democratic Party in the decades following slavery, it is important to note that "neither the Democratic nor the Republican parties of today are like their 19th century forebearers."[4]

Blacks undoubtedly played an important role in the 1900 presidential election regardless of which candidate they supported.[5] The closeness of the vote and the charges of voter fraud led to the election being challenged.[6] In Kentucky, William Jennings Bryan—the Democratic nominee trying to unseat the Republican incumbent and the eventual winner, William McKinley—won by about 8,000 votes, a 1.5% margin. Perhaps in part because of the shenanigans of local political operatives, Bryan also carried Bourbon County.

Even today politicians continue to devise unscrupulous and unethical tactics to suppress and undermine our democratic process of voting. But in the early 1900s, blacks lived under an umbrella of discriminatory practices that extended to every niche of their lives. The illicit craps game conspiracy is but one example of the widespread, intentional acts white powerbrokers pursued in that era to rob black citizens of their rights and their dignity.

Chapter 5

THE ROBBERY ATTEMPT

hat was the accusation against the 21-year-old black man that
precipitated mob violence without due process of law?

On December 5, 1900, the Paris Kentuckian-Citizen printed an article headlined "Bold Attempt at Robbery":

> *The Kentuckian-Citizen, Paris, Ky., December 5, 1900*
>
> *While Mrs. W. E. Board, wife of W. E. Board, teller
> of the Deposit Bank, of this city, was en route to her home on
> Mt. Airy Monday afternoon, about dusk, she was attacked by
> a burly negro man, who attempted to grab her pocket-book. She
> was accompanied by her young son, Lyons Board, who screamed
> manfully for help, but, after knocking Mrs. Board off her feet,
> the negro escaped before assistance arrived.*
>
> *The following is a description of the negro and should he be
> apprehended he will not fare well:*
>
> *"Brown skin, weight about 200 pounds, fairly well dressed,
> white slouch hat, pulled in at the sides, and wearing either a
> flannel shirt or a sweater."*
>
> *Mrs. Board has been prostrated with nervousness since the
> encounter.*

Some news accounts state that Mrs. W. E. Board was on her way
home from a call made to a friend in town about 6 o'clock in the evening
with her 8-year-old son, Lyons. She had just crossed the covered bridge on
2nd Street when she was assaulted by a black man.

According to the Maysville, Ky., Evening Bulletin, "Her cries and those of her son attracted the attention of some men, but the assailant escaped."[1] Some newspapers say the assailant knocked her down four times, and Mrs. Board's determined resistance and her screams frightened the assailant away. "In the semi-darkness Mrs. Board and her child obtained a good view of the negro and gave his description to the police," wrote the Courier-Journal, the Louisville, Ky., newspaper.[2]

Approximate location of the assault. Mrs. W. E. Board was en route to her home on Mt. Airy Avenue when she was assaulted after crossing the 2nd Street bridge over Houston Creek.

Chapter 6

THE MANHUNT AND AN ARREST

The police tried to identify Mrs. Board's attacker, but without avail. Then, in early February 1901, George Carter's 15-year-old sister-in-law, Bessie Smoot, filed a complaint that resulted in a warrant being issued for his arrest for attempted sexual assault.

"After long and diligent search Carter was arrested by Officer Joe Williams near Ruckerville, a negro suburb, and placed in jail," reported the Courier-Journal.[1] Upon his arrest, George was depicted as a desperate character with a bad reputation.

The following newspaper articles relay a number of inaccuracies. Records confirm that George Carter had spent one term in the state penitentiary, not two. And the alleged assault had occurred two months prior to George Carter being arrested, not three weeks. That chronological detail is important, because it shows that more time had passed between the initial incident and the attempt at identifying the perpetrator. These errors—in addition to the rumors of impending mob violence—were then perpetuated in news reports across the country.

The Daily Leader, Lexington, Ky., February 5, 1901

ON UGLY CHARGE

George Carter is Arrested at Paris. Ky.

[Special to The Leader.]
Paris, Ky., Feb. 5.—George Carter, a 20-year-old Negro, was arrested last night for attempted criminal assault on a Negro woman. Carter made an assault on the wife of Banker W. E. Board two months ago and the chances are that he will be lynched. He has served two terms in the penitentiary.

The Owensboro Messenger, Owensboro, Ky., February 7, 1901

Badly Wanted Man.

Paris, Ky., Feb. 6.—George Carter, aged twenty, colored, was arrested last night for attempted assault on a negro woman. He proved to be the same negro who, it is charged, made an assault on the wife of Banker W. E. Board two months ago. Carter has served two terms in the penitentiary.

Austin American–Statesman, Austin, Texas, February 11, 1901

MOB VIOLENCE THREATENED.

LEXINGTON, Ky., Feb. 10.—A message from Paris, Ky., states that mob violence to George Carter, colored, who was arrested Saturday for alleged attempted assault on Mrs. W. E. Board, a banker's wife, three weeks ago, in a covered bridge, is threatened. He was captured in the country.

Chapter 7

THE EXAMINING TRIAL

Georege Carter's examining trial was not for the assault on Mrs. W. E. Board, but for the warrant sworn out by Bessie Smoot, George's sister-in-law, on a charge of attempted sexual assault. The Bourbon News headline read, "Held for Attempted Assault."[1] His defense attorney was Judge Russell Mann. "The testimony showed that he had entered the room of his sister-in-law during the absence of her husband, and attempted a criminal assault upon her. The woman screamed, and the arrival of the husband prevented him from accomplishing his purpose. He was held in $300 bond to appear at the March term of the Bourbon Circuit Court."[2]

This incident might not have garnered such attention in the press except for the rumors circulating that Mr. Carter was the one who seized Mrs. W. E. Board on her way home two months before. As The Bourbon News reported, "At the present writing there is nothing positive to show that he is the party. Mrs. Board has not idedtified [sic] him. Should she do so it might be possible that the many friends of herself and husband might make an attempt to take the law into their own hands."[3]

The Bourbon News also stated that Mr. Carter had been previously incarcerated twice, once for breaking into Hedges & Walsh slaughter house and stealing lard as well as for the malicious cutting and wounding incident previously described.[4] Some newspapers said he was a member of a notorious band of negro thieves that had long terrorized Paris. The Bourbon News further stated, "There were at the time of his death three charges of attempted rape against him."[5] At the time of this writing, only the conviction of malicious cutting and wounding with intent to kill can be corroborated.

In short, the newspapers did their best to make the case against George Carter before the accuser had an opportunity to identify the accused—who had been arrested for a different charge altogether—as the one who was involved in the December 1900 incident. The wheel is set in motion for a mob's vengeful plot and for the type of justice the community seeks for Mrs. Board.

Chapter 8

THE IDENTIFICATION

Possibly the photo shown to the accuser for identification. Published in The Bourbon News, Paris, Ky., February 12, 1901.

Following George Carter's arrest, "an effort was made to secure a photograph of him at the jail, but he refused to allow it to be taken, and it was only by strategy that one was obtained. Mrs. Board, it is claimed, immediately recognized the photograph and identified it as being that of her assailant."[1] Mrs. Board's 8-year-old son, Lyons, was then taken to the jail and "fully identified the negro."[2]

As a young boy caught in the middle of a criminal matter, Lyons likely had no way of understanding the consequences of his actions and no idea what was about to unfold. After the hanging, The [Lexington] Morning Herald reported that Lyons had "been almost a nervous wreck since the affair."[3] Jennifer Taylor of the American Bar Association states,

"White people who witnessed, participated in, and socialized their children in a culture that tolerated gruesome lynchings also were psychologically damaged."[4]

The Morning Herald, Lexington, Ky., February 12, 1901

Pointing his finger at Carter he said: "That's the man that caught mamma." Carter evidently anticipated the coming of the mob after being identified by the boy, as he was heard praying aloud for ten minutes before going to bed and sang a hymn. "God be with me tonight," were the final words of his prayer as heard by his fellow prisoner. Lizzie Jackson, colored, a fellow prisoner of Carter's, said yesterday that he contemplated suicide.

"Can't you get me something to kill myself with?" he said. "They will send me to the pen for life, and I would rather be dead."

Interestingly, The Morning Herald was the only newspaper to report that Carter had confessed to assaulting Lake Board:

The Morning Herald, Lexington, Ky., February 12, 1901

Sing Kennedy and Eliza Dobbins, two negro women, friends of Bessie Smoot, told of Carter's confession to them that he had attempted to assault Mrs. Board while drunk.

Perhaps the Lexington paper had simply done more extensive re-porting than the local Paris newspapers. But a critical reader should ask: Were Bessie's two friends willing to speak falsehoods to exact vengeance on Bessie's behalf? Though the two women's story cannot be corroborat-ed, it may be relevant that Sing Kennedy was charged with murdering a woman during a jealous quarrel in 1899.[5]

Even with that reporting, it is impossible for us to know whether George Carter was indeed the man who accosted Mrs. Board near the 2nd Street bridge. No evidence was ever presented, and there was no trial. While the newspapers relay that Mrs. Board identified Carter as the per-petrator, as did her son, the description she initially gave at the time of the incident did not match Mr. Carter's physical appearance. Night was falling when the incident occurred. Nonetheless, after Mrs. Board made her identification, The Bourbon News reported that "there was no doubt in the minds of many that [Mr. Carter] would never live to stand trial, and the subsequent events of Sunday night proved that the surmises were correct."[6]

Chapter 9

FEBRUARY 11, 1901

L ess than a week after George Carter's arrest on Tuesday, February 5, 1901, for the attempted assault of his sister-in-law, he was murdered by a mob in the early morning hours of Monday, February 11. George was lynched on the 70th day following the alleged assault of Mary Lake Board.

As has been noted, the news reports surrounding these incidents were occasionally falsified or exaggerated, but they are the primary record we have. The following account of the events of that weekend has been reconstructed using those local and national newspaper sources.

By Saturday morning, February 9, rumors were flying that a lynching would occur that night. However, no one had stepped up to lead that effort, so nothing happened. The whispers continued, with the general opinion being that the lynching would now take place Monday.

But on Sunday night, February 10, the streets of Paris were empty. The electric lights had been extinguished and the town was in total darkness.

The Bourbon News reports that a lone pedestrian on his way home down 6th Street about one o'clock Monday morning noted a small procession of men and followed them out of curiosity. [*Perhaps the pedestrian was from the newspaper.*] Approximately thirty men walked rapidly down Main Street in double file. When they arrived at the county jail, they rang the bell. Jailer Allen Kiser suspected trouble and would not open the door. He peered out the window and saw the porch was crowded with men. He knew at once the meaning of the mob and endeavored to secure the keys to the cells. The mob immediately smashed the glass in the front door, opened the lock from the inside, and surged into the building.

The Bourbon County jail in Paris 1878–1939. Citizens erected this stone jail at a $15,000 cost. It was located near the old bridge on lower Main Street, which spanned Stoner Creek. [Historic Paris photos courtesy of the Hopewell Museum and The Citizen Advertiser]

The mob seized Jailer Kiser and demanded the keys. They entered Carter's cell, which was along the first corridor on the second floor,[1] and one of the men said: "Carter, we want you: you have been in here too long already."[2] Carter spoke not a word but arose to his feet. He was taken in his bare feet and thin underclothing. "The noose was thrown around his neck and he was hustled down the steps. At the foot of the steps his arms were pinioned behind him, and with a half dozen hold of the rope, and a crowd on each side and behind him, he was started up Main Street."[3]

Jailer Allen Kiser's official affidavit states:

> *"I was waked up at one o'clock. Bell rang. Went out asked who it was. Said it was Elgin [Police Officer Jeff Elgin]. Did not think it was him. Raised curtain. Saw several men dressed. Put pistol in pocket. Got keys. Then I went up stairs woke Mrs. Ashbrook up [resided in jail]. Told her was a mob down there. She got out of bed. He gave her keys. Said I will go down and talk with them. Then he heard glass smash in door burst it open. I started down stairs. They were coming up. He said don't come*

up here. Some one pointed a pistol and said come down here and give up keys and come quick. I told them I hadn't keys. They run up steps and grabbed me and pushed me down steps. Then Mrs. Ashbrook throw the keys down the hall to them. They pushed me in the office and kept me under guard. Did not see any more of it. Were they masked. Yes had handkerchiefs over face on up to one man and he was a stranger. How many. 20-25 came into the jail at first. Did not see victim any more until this morning when I saw him hanging. Goes by name of George Thomas Carter."[4]

"The other occupants of the jail, all colored, were greatly frightened and their cries and moaning could be heard several blocks," reported Maysville's newspaper.[5]

George was marched two blocks to the courthouse. "When the crowd with the trembling negro arrived at the Court House, a stop was made and the end of the rope was thrown over the iron arch at the edge of the sidewalk on which once rested so proudly the large golden eagle now placed above the balcony."[6] [*It is unknown whether the eagle was removed as part of the mob's planning or for other reasons.*]

According to The Bourbon News, "Carter was asked if he had anything to say, but whether from fear or from the fact that the rope was drawn so tight he could not speak, only a gasp issued from his lips."[7]

When Carter was first hoisted up, the rope snapped, and his body fell with a thud. Instantly another rope was produced, and the mob successfully hung him the second time. A note was then pinned on his body bearing the inscription:

"There is no place on earth for a man like this."[8]

Newspapers reported various wording for the note, but the essential message remained the same:

"This will be the fate of all negroes who assault white women."[9]

Evening Bulletin, Maysville, Ky.,
February 13, 1901

> **"THIS will be the fate of all negroes**
> **who assault white women."**
> The above is the inscription on a card
> found pinned to the body of the negro
> George Carter, who was hung by a mob
> at Paris Monday morning. It is no
> longer a question that such a fate or even
> a worse one awaits every such criminal.

The mob dispersed, and in half an hour the streets were again deserted, leaving the lifeless body swaying in the cold night air.

The Stockton (Calif.) Daily Evening Record reported, "The mob was very orderly and hardly a word was said after the victim was secured. The lynching created no excitement. The men came mostly from the country."[10]

The first person to discover the body that morning was Alfred Rice, the janitor of the courthouse, at about 5 o'clock. My grandfather Maceo Bishop said George's father was going to work at one of the mills that morning and saw a body hanging in front of the courthouse. He went to look, and to his horror, it was his son.

The acting coroner ordered the body be cut down. According to The Morning Herald, Tom Carter, George Carter's father, helped release his son from the noose.[11] Carter's body was taken to James Corbin's undertaking establishment on Main Street. A jury of about eight individuals examined the body and returned the following verdict:

> *"We the jury find the body before us to be that of George*
> *Thomas Carter, and that he came to his death on the night of*
> *February 10th at the hands of party or parties unknown."*[12]

"All morning a large crowd congregated around the body, and several enterprising amateur photographers secured snap shots of the swinging body and the crowd."[13]

Photo accompanying the article "A skeleton in Bourbon's closet," Paris Daily Enterprise, September 29, 1978.

Inquest No. _____

Received Notice *Feb. 11 1901* +89

Name *George Thomas Carter*

~~White~~. Colored. Male. ~~Female.~~

Age *21* Years *6* Months ————Days.

Nativity *American*

How Long in City *All of his life*

Married, ~~Single, Widowed~~

Occupation *Laborer*

Father's Name *Thomas Carter*

Mother's Name *Katherine Carter*

Residence *Rockerville*

Where Found *Courthouse steps*

Place of Death or Injuries *Same place*

Nature of Injuries *Hanging*

Date of Death *Feb. 11–1901*

Inquest Set *9 oclock Feb. 11–1901*

Undertaker *Corbin*

Cause of Death *Hanging*

J. H. Thomas Jr. Coroner Pro Tem

Source: Kentucky Department for Libraries & Archives, Frankfort, Ky.

VERDICT

Inquest No.

acting

I, the undersigned, Coroner of Bourbon County, having duly inquired into as to

whom and by what means   *George Thomas Carter*

whose dead body was found   *hanging on arch over gates*

leading to the Court House on the *11th* day of   *February*

A. D. *1901* , came to *his* death.

After having examined said body, and heard the evidence, I do find the deceased

came to *his* death.

*We find this to be the body of George Thomas
Carter. And find he came to his death
by hanging, by party or parties unknown
to us.*

Signed *J. W. Thomas Jr. Pro Jure* Coroner.
W. A. Parker or
W. B. Brinckazel
Rallie T. Bridwell
E. P. Bean, Jr.
J. T. Duisenbury
J. V. Muir

Source: Kentucky Department for Libraries & Archives, Frankfort, Ky.

Buffalo Evening News, Buffalo, N.Y., February 11, 1901

KENTUCKY MOB HANGS A NEGRO.

George Carter, Alleged Assailant of a White Woman, Taken From Jail at Paris and Lynched.

(By Associated Press.)

PARIS, Ky., Feb. 11.—George Carter, a negro who was in jail here charged with having assaulted Mrs. W. E. Board about three weeks ago, was lynched by a mob early this morning. Shortly after 2 o'clock about 30 determined men appeared at the jail door and demanded admittance of Jailer Kiser. He refused and the door was burst open.

The jailer was overpowered in an instant, the keys secured and in less than five minutes Carter was in the hands of the mob.

He refused to make a statement.

It was only the work of a minute to place a rope around his neck, and he was then half dragged to the entrance of the court house.

The rope was then thrown over the iron arch leading to the entrance, and, while several pulled on the rope, others lifted his body. He died by strangulation.

The mob then quietly dispersed. During the whole affair there was not a loud word spoken. Scarcely anyone in the town, outside of the immediate participants, knew that the lynching was to take place. The electric lights had previously been extinguished, and the town was in total darkness. Before the men dispersed they pinned a card on the body, bearing this inscription:

"This will be the fate of all negroes who assault white women."

The other occupants of the jail, who are all negroes, were greatly frightened, and their cries and moanings could be heard for several blocks. Half an hour after the lynching the streets were deserted and the lifeless body of the negro was swaying in the wind.

The crime with which Carter was charged was a most atrocious one. Mrs. Board, who is the wife of W. E. Board, bookkeeper at the Deposit Bank in this city, was on her way home about 6 o'clock in the evening with her little son, when she was assaulted by a negro. Her cries and those of her son attracted the attention of some men, but the assailant escaped.

Constant efforts were made by the police to detect the negro, but without avail until last week, when Bessie Smoot of Ruckerville, caused a warrant to be issued for George Carter, her brother-in-law, on a charge of assault.

A photograph of him was obtained, which, it is said, Mrs. Board identified as being that of her assailant and at the county jail her little son also identified him.

Stockton Daily Evening Record, Stockton, Calif., February 11, 1901

JUDGE LYNCH AGAIN

This Time It Is In Kentucky.

George Carter, a Negro, Who Assaulted Mrs. W. E. Board.

Special to the Record.

PARIS, Ky., February 11.—George Carter, a negro, who has been in jail here several days on a charge of having assaulted Mrs. W. E. Board, was lynched at an early hour this morning.

Shortly before daybreak a mob of forty men appeared at the jail and demanded the keys. These were refused and the mob proceeded to break in the doors. A rope was thrown over the negro and he was dragged across the street and strung up in front of the Courthouse, a projecting beam from that building being used for the gibbet.

He was offered an opportunity to make a statement, but he refused to say anything.

The mob was very orderly and hardly a word was said after the victim was secured. The lynching created no excitement. The men came mostly from the country.

The Daily Leader, Lexington, Ky., February 12, 1901,
referencing the Cincinnati Commercial Tribune

The following from The Commercial Tribune of course puts an entirely different phase on the lynching: But, the fact remains that the very orderly and gentlemanly small, but select, Paris, Ky., mob lynched Negro George Carter not for his assault upon his sister-in-law, of like sable hue, but for alleged perpetration of a more remote outrage upon a victim of Caucasian complexion.

Theodore Roosevelt Jr. (1858–1919), circa 1904 [Wikipedia], the 26th Presdent of the United States, 1901–1909

Two and a half years following the lynching of George Carter, President Theodore Roosevelt expressed "his own views in reference to lynching and mob violence, generally, pointing out that mob violence is merely one form of anarchy and that anarchy is the forerunner of tyranny."[14]

The Bourbon News, Paris, Ky., August 11, 1903

"All thoughtful men," says the president, "must feel the gravest alarm over the growth of lynching in this country, and especially over the peculiarly hideous form so often taken by mob violence when colored men are the victims—on which occasions the mob seems to lay most weight, not on the crime, but on the color of the criminal."

Chapter 10

ATTEMPTED ROBBERY VS. RAPE

Newspapers across America that printed the George Carter story expressed a similar sentiment, "The crime with which Carter was charged was a most atrocious one."[1] The crime, which was initially reported as an attempted robbery, somehow morphed into something more heinous. Through unscrupulous reporting by newspapers, readers were led to believe that the assault was an attempted rape, contradicting the initial report.

The Kentuckian Citizen, Paris, Ky., December 5, 1900

BOLD ATTEMPT AT ROBBERY.

While Mrs. W. E. Board, wife of W. E. Board, teller of the Deposit Bank, of this city, was en route to her home on Mt. Airy Monday afternoon, about dusk, she was attacked by a burly negro man, who attempted to grab her pocket-book. She was accompanied by her young son, Lyons Board, who screamed manfully for help, but, after knocking Mrs. Board off her feet, the negro escaped before assistance arrived.

The following is a description of the negro and should he be apprehended he will not fare well:

"Brown skin, weight about 200 pounds, ... well dressed, white slouch hat, ... in at the sides, and wearing ... a flannel shirt or a sweater."

... Board has been prostrated with ... since the encounter.

The Marion Star, Marion, Ohio, February 11, 1901

A RAPIST LYNCHED AT PARIS

George Carter, a Negro Who Commits an Assault on Mrs. Lake Board Three Weeks Ago, Is Hanged By a Kentucky Mob Early This Morning.

Keys of the Jail Are Demanded from the Sheriff--He Refuses To Give Them Up, but Is Overpowered--Prisoner, Asked To Plead, Remains Silent.

Paris, Ky., Feb. 11.—George Carter, a negro, who assaulted Mrs. Lake Board, about three weeks ago, was taken from the county jail at 2 o'clock this morning by a mob of fifty determined men and hanged to an iron arch in front of the court house.

The Mount Vernon (Ky.) Signal declared, "It is passingly strange, indeed, that those brutes in human form, will never learn that as long as such crimes are committed, death will swiftly pay the penalty, and very often in horrid form....The North raise a great cry every time one of those brutes is swung up for this crime; but when one of them dares molest a white woman on the northern banks of the Ohio, he may as well say his prayers – he is a goner."[2]

The term *rape* was used to provoke and enrage law-abiding citizens, particularly when the crime was committed by a black man against a white woman. Chloe Angyal writes, "The defense of white womanhood was, in the recent past, used as a justification for the most horrific violence against black people, and particularly black men."[3] In contrast, rape of a black woman by a white male was common, and there was little legal recourse for the victim during that era.

"All that being said, white women, and a particular way of thinking about white womanhood, were central to the practice of lynching," wrote Jessie Daniels.[4]

Distorting the crime into attempted rape, in the minds of many, justified the mob's swift action and the punishment meted.

Kentucky Lynchings 1882 - 1921

Originally Researched by Rob Gallagher

Further Research done by Lori DeWinkler of Genealogy Trails to confirm the accuracy of this list.

ST #	VICTIM	RACE	SEX	OFFENSE	MO	DAY	YEAR	COUNTY	STATE
97	Carter, George	Blk	Male	Atempted rape	Feb	11	1901	Bourbon	KY

[Source: Rob Gallagher and Lori DeWinkler, "Kentucky Genealogy Trails" (excerpt), http://genealogytrails.com/ken/ky_southernlynchings.html]

Chapter 11

DÉJÀ VU

The Gloversville, N.Y., front-page headline read, "ANOTHER LYNCHING IN PARIS, KENTUCKY." For many older Bourbon County residents, the Carter hanging must have elicited a sense of déjà vu. Just twelve years earlier another mob had lynched James (Jim) Kelly under similar circumstances.

GLOVERSVILLE, N. Y., MONDAY, FEBRUARY 11, 1901.

VOL. XIV, NO. 143

ANOTHER LYNCHING IN PARIS, KENTUCKY

On July 25, 1889, an accusation of rape was made by 27-year-old Mary Crow, formerly Mary Berry of Nicholas County. She was the wife of Peter Crow, a section boss on the Kentucky Central railroad. It is interesting to note that Jim Kelly worked for Mary's husband, Peter. As co-workers, it is assumed that Jim and Peter knew each other well at the time of the alleged rape. Also, it is possible that through Peter, Jim and Mary were at least casually acquainted. The papers stated that Jim had come to Paris, Ky., about four years earlier from Virginia.

The Daily Leader's account stated that Jim went to the house of Peter Crow and found no one at home with Mrs. Crow. "He made an attempt to rape her but did not succeed until he had kept up his attempt for more than three hours. He finally knocked her down, held her by the throat with one hand, and held a pistol in her face with the other, and accomplished his purpose."[1] Before leaving the house, Mrs. Crow said she scratched his face so that he could be easily recognized.

On the day following the assault, the lynch mob sent a committee to the home of Mary Crow to determine the facts. Upon the committee's return, it was reported that she was raped and in very critical condition. This report sealed Jim Kelly's fate and within a few hours, approximately 100 men stormed the jail and dragged Kelly from the jail to the place where he was hung, a bridge near town.[2]

Louisville's Courier-Journal wrote, "He [Jim] at first refused to talk, but finally denied the charge, as was expected he would."[3] Jim was described by the Lexington Daily Leader as a large, burly negro, weighing over 200 pounds. Ironically, this is the same description The Kentuckian-Citizen reported for the man who attempted to rob Mary Lake Board twelve years later. It was also said that Jim had a "bad reputation," but no specifics were provided to support that assertion.

Buried in the details of this account, the Courier-Journal provided some additional Bourbon County history: "A negro was hung here in 1867, in broad daylight, in the Court-house yard, for raping an eleven-year-old daughter of a Mr. Doolin."[4]

The Courier-Journal concluded with its own verdict of Jim's hanging: "The verdict of the people is that the hanging was a just one."[5] The excitement in the city of Paris was intense. "Not a man can be found of any standing who does not say that the people were lenient in hanging the perpetrator of this foulest crime within the range of criminal jurisprudence," reported The Kentucky Leader.[6]

Altoona Tribune, Altoona, Pa., July 27, 1889

Lynched Yesterday Morning.

PARIS, Ky., July 26.—At 2 o'clock this morning seventy-five men called at the jail and rapped on the door, saying they had a prisoner. The jailor threw the doors open when the mob rushed in, overpowering the jailor and his deputy. The men went to the cell of Jim Kelly, the negro who assaulted the wife of Peter Crow, yesterday, took him and placed a rope around his neck. The negro was then taken to the railroad bridge and ordered to step off, which he did, and fell four feet, dying from strangulation.

Kelly was from Virginia, and had been working on the railroad four years, and was in the employ of Crow, the section boss. He had a bad reputation. Mrs. Crow, his victim, is a handsome woman and is prostrated by the shock. After committing the crime Kelly hung around the house and played the innocent, but he had two pistols on his person. The mob were armed with shotguns, picks, clubs, etc., and stationed pickets from the jail to the bridge, a half mile distant. The body hung until 7 o'clock this morning, when the coroner cut it down. Kelly admitted his guilt once, but afterward protested his innocence.

Kentucky Lynchings 1882 - 1921

Originally Researched by Rob Gallagher

Further Research done by Lori DeWinkler of Genealogy Trails to confirm the accuracy of this list.

ST #	VICTIM	RACE	SEX	OFFENSE	MO	DAY	YEAR	COUNTY	STATE
40	Kelly, James	Blk	Male	Rape	Jul	26	1889	Bourbon	KY

[Source: Rob Gallagher and Lori DeWinkler, "Kentucky Genealogy Trails" (excerpt), http://genealogytrails.com/ken/ky_southernlynchings.html]

A few days after Jim Kelly was lynched, the Lexington Daily Leader reported: "It is a singular coincidence that the very evening Mrs. Crow was being so brutally treated by the negro near Paris, her cousins were trying to kill her brother. Six of them paraded around our train at Carlisle depot with guns."

The Kentucky Leader, Lexington, Ky., July 31, 1889

SINGULAR COINCIDENCE.

The Berrys and Shannons at War in Carlisle and Hunting Each Other with Guns.

Paris Kentuckian-Citizen.

The Berrys and Shannons, who had the fight last Wednesday near Carlisle, were held over Monday in bonds of $500 each. There were three Berrys, sons of Pat Berry, and two Shannons against two Berrys, sons of Martin Berry. The difficulty was caused some time ago by Shannon and Martin Berry's son being suitors for the hand of Miss Crow. Martin Berry's son is a brother of Mrs. Crow, and Miss Crow a sister of Mrs. Peter Crow. It is a singular coincidence that the very evening Mrs. Crow was being so brutally treated by the negro near Paris, her cousins were trying to kill her brother. Six of them paraded around our train at Carlisle depot with guns.

As with the lynching of George Carter twelve years later, the circumstances surrounding Jim Kelly's lynching are suspect and questionable. The accounts of newspapers across America varied, with significant discrepancies and purposeful distortions. Unfortunately, the truth behind this injustice will never be known, forever buried under more than a century of time.

Chapter 12

A REWARD FOR APPREHENSION OF LYNCHERS

An African American organization in Seattle, Wash.—The International Council of the World—offered a reward of $500 for the apprehension and conviction of each and every person connected with the lynching of George Carter.[1] The Council was an antilynching organization that had a million members and $1,000,000 to expend until mob violence ceased. Samuel Burdett (c. 1846–1905), a remarkable African American pioneer born in Kentucky, helped organize the Council in 1901.[2]

This Committee met on February 11, 1901, and transacted the following business with regards to the lynching of George Carter:

> *"WHEREAS, It has come to our knowledge that one George Carter was, on the 10th day of February, 1901, at Paris, Kentucky, hung to death and murdered, by mob violence, and without due process of law, and believing the same to be true, now therefore be it*
>
> *RESOLVED, that it is the sense of this council, and it is ordered, that the authorized attorney of this organization is hereby directed to prepare in legal form, an offer of a reward of five hundred dollars (500) for the apprehension and conviction of each and every person whatsoever implicated in the murder of said George Carter, as aforesaid; and that the Secretary be instructed to forward one copy of this resolution to the Governor of the State of Kentucky; one copy to the Chief of Police of the City of Paris;*

one copy to the Sheriff of Bourbon County, Kentucky, at once; and that these resolutions be spread upon the minutes of this International Council; and be it further

RESOLVED, That it is the duty of, and it is enjoined upon, each and every Supreme and Subordinate Council throughout the United States, to co-operate to their fullest ability in the carrying out of this resolution, to the end that the perpetrators of said murder may be brought to justice, and that the ends of the law may be subserved.

(seal)
Samuel Burbelt [sic], Pres.
J. L. Gibson, Sec." [3]

This typewritten letter was met with disdain by its recipients, Paris' sheriff and chief of police, as reflected in The Bourbon News headline: "Small Concern With a Big Name." No legal action ever resulted from the murder of George Thomas Carter.

Chapter 13

THE IRONY

There is irony in this tragedy. George was hung from the arched gate that stood sentinel in the Bourbon County Courthouse's shadow. Injustice prevailed where justice should have flourished. In the United States, the courthouse represents a place where the defendant stands innocent until proven guilty. It contains law courts where proceedings are held to protect our constitutional rights to equal protection and due process under the law. It is where a case is heard by neutral judges and/or juries. During this era, however, as George C. Wright relays, "laws were stringently applied to blacks, and they were often convicted of offenses for which whites would not even have been charged."[1]

Resting above the balcony of the Courthouse in 1901 was a large golden eagle, America's symbol of this nation's independence and the freedom afforded its citizens. The eagle represents courage, honesty, and truth. Yet as the worlds of George Carter and Mary Lake Board collided, the scale of justice tilted, unevenly, away from George. His life was fraught with discrimination, while Lake enjoyed a life of privilege. Ultimately, the search for truth was superseded by expediency and illegitimate power. Justice was not served. Freedom was extinguished.

Chapter 14

OMINOUS WORDS

The Bourbon News expressed its disapproval of lynch law, saying "the laws of the country are strong enough to adequately punish any violator of them."[1] However, it also allowed for extenuating circumstances, particularly if white women were threatened. According to George C. Wright, most whites during that era depicted lynchers as sincere people forced to take the law into their own hands to ensure that their civilization was not destroyed by blacks.[2]

In addition to editorializing its position on lynching, The Bourbon News published the following communication from H. W. Conrad, a Bourbon County physician, the day after George Carter was hung:

> *"If every newspaper would speak as strongly against the mob spirit, it would soon lessen. Every scoundrel who commits such a deed, regardless of the color of either victim or assaulter, should be given the extreme penalty of the law; but no mobs. The mob spirit is spreading too rapidly in this country. The victims of it are no longer confined to one race nor mobbed for the one crime, nor confined to one section of the country. It is becoming both fashionable and popular. If this disregard for law, for the fullest investigation by judge and jury, be not stopped, the logical sequence may be but one thing—**eventually the burning of Court Houses**, the lynching of judges and other public officials. The mob may even lay its sacrilegious hands upon editors."[3]*

Chapter 15

THE BOURBON COURTHOUSE

Dr. H. W. Conrad's words were pregnant with meaning and resounded through the months following George Carter's lynching. Conrad expressed concern that lynching could eventually lead to other crimes, such as the burning of courthouses.

Eight months after the lynching of George Carter, the Bourbon County Courthouse was destroyed by fire. No criminal act was involved; investigators determined that a defective flue started a blaze in the ceiling of the Circuit Court room. In an hour the building was in ruins. At 11:20 a.m. on October 19, 1901, the big tower fell, seemingly unable to bear the shame of the injustice that had befallen George Carter. Only the courthouse walls were left standing.

Though it had been a beautiful structure, after George Carter's lynching the courthouse evolved into a symbol of injustice for the black community. Black residents were beset with frustration and anger over his senseless murder and the abject fear that fell upon them. Through a time of dampened hope, they relied on their religion to sustain them. Following slavery, religion remained an integral part of the life of African Americans. When the courthouse burned down, some in the black community felt its destruction was comeuppance, a reaping of the ugly seeds of hatred planted that horrid day when Carter was murdered.

Thus, in Paris' history, two incidents in 1901 are forever linked: the lynching of George Carter at the courthouse gate and the courthouse fire. As in one breath the events were re-told by my grandfather: A black man was lynched in front of the Courthouse and then the Courthouse burned down.[1]

The third Bourbon County Courthouse, a grand French Renaissance-style building, was erected in 1873 at a cost of $130,000. It had a clock and bell tower rising 113 feet into the sky and was considered one of the handsomest and best-appointed structures of its kind in the state. An iron fence was all around. "It was a historic structure, all the noted Kentuckians in their days having spoken within its walls."[2] [Photo courtesy of the Hopewell Museum]

After the fire, October 19, 1901. [Photo courtesy of the Hopewell Museum]

The Courier-Journal, Louisville, Ky., October 20, 1901

BOURBON COUNTY COURTHOUSE IS DESTROYED BY FLAMES

The Building Is a Complete Wreck, Only the Walls Being Left Standing---The Records Safe.

Paris, Ky., Oct. 19.—[Special.]—A defective flue started a blaze in the ceiling of the Circuit Court room in the Paris courthouse this morning and in an hour the building was in ruins. The alarm was given about 10:45 o'clock, when Albert Rice, the janitor, noticed dense volumes of smoke pouring from the Circuit Court room. The fire department responded promptly, but its work was badly handicapped by poor water pressure, and a lack of ladders to reach the seat of the fire. Fanned by a strong wind, the fire spread rapidly, and in forty minutes the building from the first story to the top of the tower was a mass of flames. At 11:20 o'clock the big tower fell, carrying with it the heavy slate roof and the upper floor and completing the wreck. Only the walls are left standing.

The Lexington fire department responded to a telegraphic call, but could render no aid on account of the poor water facilities. The records in the various offices are thought to be safe, as they were in fire-proof vaults, but are possibly slightly damaged by smoke or water. Several narrow escapes were made by firemen from being crushed by the falling floors and cornices.

The building was erected in 1872 at a cost of $145,000, and was considered one of the handsomest and best appointed structures of its kind in the State. There is $52,500 insurance on the house, and $7,000 on the furniture. The old building was burned in 1871. It was a historic structure, all the noted Kentuckians in their days having spoken within its walls.

County officers will open temporary quarters in adjacent buildings.

Today the salvaged iron gate stands adjacent to the historic Duncan Tavern, just west of the new Bourbon County Courthouse. A few years ago a new eagle, designed by artist Adalin Wichman, replaced the original eagle.

Duncan Tavern in the early 1900s. The courthouse would be just to the right of the photo. [Photo courtesy of Ted Wiseman]

Chapter 16

ANTILYNCHING LEGISLATION

Following the lynching of George Carter in 1901, "Judge Lynch" continued to rear its ugly head throughout Kentucky, including more incidents in Bourbon County.

Early Saturday morning on August 28, 1914, Bourbon County Jailer Joseph Farris routed a mob of about 25 men after killing one and perhaps badly wounding another.[1] Farris was trying to protect a prisoner in his keeping: Henry Johnson, a black man from Illinois. The Bourbon News initially reported that Johnson entered a Paris home and attacked the wife of Henry Meade. However, Henry Meade's account later differed from the News' story, which was obviously intent on inciting the public. According to Meade, he returned home one night and found the negro in his house. A trial was held, and Henry Johnson was sentenced to two years in the penitentiary for housebreaking.

Richmond Daily Register, Richmond, Ky.,
March 30, 1920

MOB MAKES QUICK WORK OF RAPIST

Negro Who Assaulted Little Girl, Taken From Officers At Paris and Hanged

---

(By Associated Press)

Maysville, Ky., Mar. 30—The body of Grant Smith, the negro, aged 40, confessed assailant of Ruby Anderson, 14, daughter of Robert Anderson, of Johnson Junction, hanged by a mob near Flemingsburg last night, was cut down today. His hat was still on the head. The body was not mutilated. Officers from whom the mob took Smith, are not subject to the new state law which vacates the office of those who permit mobs to take prisoners. The bill was signed by the Governor but because it carries no emergency clause, is not effective until June 1st.

In March 1920, another Bourbon County mob lynched Grant Smith, a black man accused of assaulting a white girl. On April 2, 1920, The Bourbon News reported, "The coroner's jury returned a verdict stating that Grant Smith, negro, lynched on the Maysville pike for alleged assault on a girl, met death at hands of persons unknown. Deputy Sheriff George W. Powell, from whom the negro was taken at Paris, said on his arrival at Flemingsburg, Tuesday, that he was unable to identify any of the members of the mob."[2]

The newspaper went on to say that Kentucky Gov. Edwin P. Morrow remained up until long past midnight awaiting definite word from Fleming County, where Grant Smith was lynched. The state legislature had passed a law in February requiring the removal from office of peace officers who surrender their prisoners to mobs. The Governor declared that while the law is still inoperative (it didn't take effect until June 1920), the law had been passed to suppress mob violence. The law explicitly states that, "Any person who takes part in a mob shall be guilty of lynching and the penalty for lynching is death or imprisonment."[3]

"The incident is most regrettable," said the Governor, "and the law should have been allowed to take its course."[4]

Though lynching did not end in Kentucky with these incidents, Kentucky's governors and the state legislature showed a growing commitment to combat lawlessness in the early 1900s. "Thus Kentucky became the first southern state to pass an antilynching law," wrote J. D. Wright.[5]

Chapter 17

THE AFTERMATH

Two households forever remain tucked in the shadows of that horrendous wintry night: the Carters and the Boards. The lynching of George Carter was history. What happened to those families in the months and years that followed?

George's Sister-in-law Bessie

Bessie had her own problems with the law. Two years after the lynching she was arrested and fined $20.75 for running a "joint" in Ruckerville. Life was not easy for Bessie, who had a second-grade education and was, thus, illiterate. Desperation sometimes leads to unlawful choices.

The Bourbon News, Paris, Ky., February 10, 1903

> ·ARRESTED —Carrie Collier and Bessie Smoot, colored, were fined $20.75 each, in Judge Smith's court, Saturday, for running a "joint" in Ruckerville.

When she married William Henry Smoot in April 1900, Bessie was a 15-year-old girl. Before reaching her first wedding anniversary, she swore out a warrant to have her brother-in-law, George Carter, arrested. Nothing could have prepared her for what happened next. Six days after his arrest on February 5, 1901, George was lynched for reasons unrelated to her sworn warrant. One can only speculate whether Bessie was impacted psychologically by those events. "Many black women were reluctant to report their sexual victimization by black men for fear that the black men would be lynched," wrote Deborah G. White.[1] Bessie faced an ordeal that required mental and emotional capacities beyond her years.

In the years that followed, Bessie struggled to find her footing in life. By the 1930 census, she and her third husband, John Parker, had relocated from Ohio to Detroit, Mich., where she died as a widow in 1946 at age 61. No record was found of any surviving children.

George's Wife and Children

George's wife, Mary Eliza, was undoubtedly traumatized after he was lynched. To compound her sense of loss, there was likely a feeling of betrayal for the attempted sexual assault of her younger sister, Bessie Smoot, the incident that had landed George in jail. As a widow and single parent of two daughters under the age of three, Mary Eliza faced the responsibility of providing for her young family.

Did tension exist between Mary Eliza and her sister Bessie? The answer is unknown, but the family needed a fresh start to heal and, perhaps more importantly, opportunities for employment. As George C. Wright explains, "The discrimination that Afro-Americans faced in virtually every area of employment led many of them to leave the state for what they believed would be better job opportunities in the North."[2] Mary Eliza's family, the Thompsons, along with Mary Eliza and her daughters, eventually left Bourbon County, relocating to Columbus, Ohio.

Mary Eliza fell in love again and married William Pierce, who was also a native Kentuckian. By the 1920 census, she was living with her husband in the household of her brother William Thompson and other lodgers in Columbus. She eventually moved to Ironton, Ohio, where she lived the remainder of her life. Tragically Mary Eliza Pierce died at age 53 in November 1932 from burns sustained in an accident in her home.

Residing with Mary Eliza at the time of her death were her husband and younger daughter, Carrie. By this time Carrie was separated from her second husband, John Sinkford. Sinkford had killed a local minister with whom Carrie was having a year-long affair. Sinkford was exonerated after Carrie testified on his behalf, confirming the affair.

Ohio marriage record of John Sinkford and Carrie Carter, younger daughter of George Carter.

Carrie spent the last few years of her life as a scorned woman in the Ironton community. Her actions—and those of her husband—had led to the death of a beloved minister who was widely known in church circles throughout the state. Tragically, both she and her Aunt Bessie had made decisions that paved the path for a man's murder.

The Cincinnati Enquirer, Cincinnati, Ohio,
October 19, 1927

HUSBAND IS EXONERATED.

SPECIAL DISPATCH TO THE ENQUIRER.

Ironton, Ohio, October 19.—John Sinkford, negro, who shot and killed Rev. O. A. Williams, negro, was exonerated of a second-degree murder charge today after a jury had considered his case for five hours. Mrs. Sinkford testified for her husband and admitted that the preacher had been a caller at their home several times weekly for a year.

Carrie died of a heart condition at age 35, only three years following her mother's death.

George's older daughter, Lillie Mae, survived a life of heartache. In addition to losing her father as a 2-year-old toddler, she mourned the tragic death of her mother as well as the deaths of her sister, Carrie, two daughters, and her first husband, Tom.

Lillie Mae was only 15 when she married Randolph Thomas (Tom) Hill in February 1914 in Lawrence, Ohio. By 1920 the Hill family had relocated to Logan, W. Va., where Lillie Mae was employed as a cook in a private home and her husband was a coal miner. Within seven years of their marriage, five children were born to their union: Frances, William, Hannah, Katherine, and Addie. Two children predeceased Lillie Mae: Addie died at age 6 from accidental burns, and Katherine died at age 15 due to acute nephritis related to a pregnancy.

In 1938 Lillie Mae married William (Bill) Fields, also a coal miner. Both were widows when they married. The 1940 census includes their 1-year-old daughter, Sarah Ann.

On December 22, 1973, Lillie Mae Carter Fields, age 75, died in Logan, W.Va.

Marriage license for Lillie Mae and her second husband, William Fields, in 1938.

George's Parents

Unlike the Thompson family, George's parents—Tom and Kate—remained in Paris. The source of their grief was twofold: the brutal murder of their oldest child and the separation from their two granddaughters, Lillie Mae and Carrie, who relocated with their mother to Ohio. It's probable that Tom and Kate never laid eyes on them again after they departed Bourbon County.

There's a hole that's hard to fill when a loved one dies, but Tom and Kate persevered and focused on being good parents to their three surviving children. Sadly, their daughter Ora Lee also predeceased them in 1917. In the 1910 census, Ora Lee and her husband, Jasper Johnson, had a 3-year-old daughter named Margret, but no record is found of her in the following census. She possibly predeceased Ora Lee.

The Bourbon News, Paris, Ky., December 25, 1917

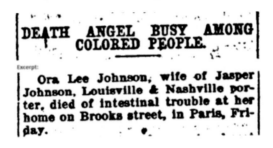

DEATH ANGEL BUSY AMONG COLORED PEOPLE.

Excerpt:

Ora Lee Johnson, wife of Jasper Johnson, Louisville & Nashville porter, died of intestinal trouble at her home on Brooks street, in Paris, Friday.

During Tom's lifetime, he worked diligently to support his wife and children. "In consideration of one dollar ($1.00) cash in hand paid, and love and affection" which he had for his children, Tom granted and conveyed his two homes on Brooks Street to the surviving children.

```
1936.                    THOMAS CARTER.
JAN.                       TO   LOT   $1.        |||||||||||||||||||||
15.                      KATIE CARTER.                 3 25 788

        THIS DEED, made and entered into this 15th. day of January, 1936, by and

   between Thomas Carter, a single person, of Paris, Kentucky, party of the first

   part, and Katie Carter, his daughter of Paris, Kentucky, party of the second part,

        WITNESSETH: That said party of the first part for and in consideration of

   the sum of One ($1.00) Dollar, and the love and affection he bears to the party of

   the second part, who is his daughter, has bargained and sold and does hereby grant

   and convey unto the party of the second part, her heirs and assigns forever, the

   following described property located in the city of Paris, Bourbon County, Ken-

   tucky, and described as follows, to-wit:-

        Lot #10 in Brooks Addition to the city of Paris in Bourbon County, Kentucky,
   fronting fifty (50) feet on the east side of Brooks Street, and extending back
   therefrom to Turney's line, a distance of one hundred and fifteen (115) feet, more
   or less, and is same width throughout. Said lot is bounded on the North by lot #9
   sold to Milby Parker and south by lot #11. And being the same property conveyed
   to Thomas Carter, party of the first part, by W. T. Brooks and wife, by deed of
   date the 20th. day of August, 1891, and recorded in the Bourbon County Clerk's
   office in Deed Book  77 page 526.

        To have and to hold the same with all the appurtenances thereon unto the

   said second party, her heirs and assigns forever, with covenant of General Warrant.

        In testimony whereof witness my signature this 15th. day of January, 1936.

                                                    his
   Attest: Neville C. Fisher.              Thomas X Carter.
                                                    mark
```

Excerpt of 1936 deed in which Tom Carter sold property to daughter Katie for $1.00.

George's siblings also remained in Paris. Some years later, in the early 1940s, Willie relocated with his wife and children to Springfield, Ohio. George's mother, Kate, died in 1934; his father, Tom, died nine years later in 1943.

The Board Family

Following the lynching of George Carter, life for the Board family resumed much as it had prior to the incident. The Bourbon News voraciously reported the Boards' comings and goings between 1897 and 1913. The popular couple hosted many guests in their homes and traveled throughout Kentucky visiting family and friends. During their marriage, the Boards enjoyed life amid Paris' best social circles, attending tea parties and dances as well as events sponsored by the Darby and Joan Club, the Euchre Club, and the Bourbon Bridge Club.

Following are examples of the busy social life of Mrs. W. E. (Mary Lake) Board.

The Bourbon News, Paris, Ky., January 5, 1906

—Mrs. W. E. Board entertained the Bourbon Bridge Club yesterday afternoon, and will entertain the Jemima Johnson Chapter. D. A. R., this afternoon.

The Bourbon News, Paris, Ky., November 24, 1911

—One of the most beautiful parties of the season was the tea Mrs. W. E. Board gave Tuesday in honor of Mrs. P. H. Lane, of Philadelphia, guest of Mrs. Swift Champ. The home was attractively decorated in smilax, ferns and handsome white chrysanthemums, and was lighted with many candles in silver and crystal candelabra.

In the receiving line with Mrs. Board was Mrs. Lane and Mrs. Rebecca Hughes. Mrs. Lane's gown was imported lace robe over yellow messaline. Mrs. Board wore a lovely gown of lavendar crepe. Mrs. Hughes wore black crepe de chine.

Mrs. E. M. Dickson presided at the tea table and Mrs. Jas. Wilson poured hot chocolate in the dining room where the decorations were especially beautiful. About seventy five guests were present.

The Bourbon News, Paris, Ky., August 23, 1912

—Mrs. W. E. Board entertained delightfully yesterday afternoon at her home on Mt. Airy avenue with a beautiful luncheon auction-bridge for Mrs. Gertrude Warner, of Lagrange. There were four tables and at each table was a silver picture frame, the prizes, while the prize for the guest of honor was a picture frame of large pattern. Following the several interesting games an elaborate luncheon was served the guests.

The Winchester News, Winchester, Ky.,
February 26, 1909

BOURBON ATTORNEYS
BUSY FILING SUITS.

Non-Resident Firms Seek to Collect
From North Middletown
Concern.

PARIS, Ky., Feb. 26.—A number of suits were filed yesterday in the Bourbon circuit court and as tomorrow is the last day that such suits can be filed, local attorneys will be quite busy.

Judge Harmon Stitt, as attorney for L. Frank, doing business as Frank & Company, filed two suits, one against W. E. Board, on a promissory note for $100, dated July 10, 1903, and against W. W. Cherry for recovery on an account to the amount of $131.64.

Though Lake grew up in a financially stable home, married life to Bill was occasionally financially challenging. His "personal financial affairs always seemed in unseemly disarray. He would buy and sell parcels of land around town and sign bank notes for the questionable activities of his brother."[3] The family faced several legal suits from local businesses seeking to collect money. One of those suits was filed in 1909 by Frank & Company for a $100 promissory note dated July 10, 1903.

The Boards were also sued by Lavin & Connell, a retail grocer located at the northwest corner of 8th and Main. Items purchased by Mary Lake Board were largely groceries: flour, bacon cheese, fruits, vegetables, lard, spaghetti, almonds, coffee, tea, chocolate, eggs, pickles. The grocer filed a suit in February 1908 for purchases between 1904 and 1906 totaling $426.49. Only a small portion had been re-paid.

Paris merchant J. T. Hinton sued the Boards as well. J. T. Hinton sold furniture, carpets, wallpaper, window treatments, and other household goods. The suit was filed in May 1908 for goods, merchandise, and labor totaling $131.69.

Excerpt of Mrs. W. E. Board's cumulative bill from merchant J. T. Hinton, who sued the Boards in 1908 for non-payment.

Summons filed against the Boards by merchant J. T. Hinton in 1908.

Fortunately for Lake, her father, Dr. L. D. Barnes, had had the foresight to protect her inheritance. An excerpt from Dr. Barnes' 1879 Last Will and Testament, written before Lake married Bill Board, states: "The portion going to our daughter Mary Lake Barnes to be held & managed by a Trustee for her own use and benefit, free from control of any husband she may ever have."

Despite their financial woes, the Boards provided their son, Lyons, with an excellent education, sending him to the private academy taught by Professor T. B. Threlkeld in Nicholasville, Ky. After completing his studies, he held various positions at businesses in Paris, including Price & Co. Clothing and C. B. Mitchell's dry goods store, before moving to Lagrange, Ky., where he worked at McDowell Drug Company. In 1913 he had "a responsible position with the drug firm of H. H. Sprague & Co., at Middlesboro."[4]

Bill also changed careers. He eventually left his bookkeeping position with the Deposit Bank and joined Unity Insurance of Pittsburgh, a job that required extensive travel to Cincinnati, Louisville, Covington, Newport, and Knoxville. Some stays lasted up to six weeks.

The Bourbon News, Paris, Ky., November 8, 1912

New Art Store!

I will open an Art Store on or before the 15th of November in the store room next to Mrs. M. A. Paton. New and fresh stock of all kinds of fancy work—

Embroidery,

Pillow Cases,

Towels,

Underwear,

Waists, Etc.

Novelties of all Kinds

Stamping Done on Short Notice — Everything guaranteed to be the best. : : ; : : : :

Mrs. W. E. Board

Beginning October 1912, the local newspaper reported that Mr. W. E. (Bill) Board was quite ill and confined to his home. A few weeks after this report, Lake advertised the opening of her art store, where she sold embroidered and stamped finery and gifts. This was probably her first foray into earning income for her family. She leaned on her social connections and her experience entertaining guests, transforming her knack for artful home decorating and gift design into a business.

By 1914 Bill had become an invalid and his illness had led to blindness and paralysis, leaving him helpless. He had numerous hospitalizations in Massie Memorial Hospital in Paris and Eastern State Hospital in Lexington.

Lake eventually gave up her art store in 1917 and moved to Louisville where she accepted a position as a house mother for the young nurses at the Norton Infirmary. Bill died on January 31, 1918, at Eastern State. His cause of death was listed as "General paralysis of the insane" from the effects of syphilis.[5]

In March 1918, the grief of Bill's death was still fresh when Lake received news that her son, Lyons, had been inducted into the army. That summer he was transferred from Camp Zachary Taylor outside Louisville to Camp Sherman near Chillicothe, Ohio, where he was assigned to duty at the camp hospital. He served in the infantry in France from September 1918 until April 1919.

The Bourbon News, Paris, Ky., November 8, 1918

✚ ✚ ✚

A postcard from Private Lyons
Board, formerly of Paris, who is now
in France, says:

"I am a long way from Paris (Ky.),
but I am going to start for old Kentucky sooner than you people at home
think for. Regards to all." The re-
verse side of the card shows an im-
mense lot of eight-inch shells, packed
ten or twelve in a row, being in-
spected by Gen. Pershing and staff,
with the motto: "We shoot this many
shells at the Huns every few seconds.
Liberty Bonds will buy more!"

✚ ✚ ✚

Upon release from military service in 1919, Lyons traveled to Paris, Ky., on a combined business and pleasure trip, still intending to make Louisville his future home. Many in Paris mistakenly believed that Lyons had served in battle with the 110th Field Signal Corps, which was referred to as "The Suicide Club" and lauded for its exceptional bravery, as had been reported by The Bourbon News. In actuality, Lyons hadn't been assigned to that battalion until after the Armistice was signed.[6]

The granddaughter of William Lyons Board stumbled across this photo in a box of old pictures belonging to her mother. Though the figure is not identified, it is possible this is Lyons during World War I.

The Bourbon News, Paris, Ky., May 20, 1919

One of the latest arrivals in the old home town for a few days' visit was private Lyons Board, formerly of Paris and Louisville, from which place he enlisted in the service. Private Board was a member of the 110th Field Signal Corps, familiarly referred to as "The Suicide Club," on account of their being assigned to duty on the extreme outposts in time of war. The 110th was a part of the Thirty-fifth Division, which saw nine months active field service in France. Mr. Board has received his honorable discharge at Camp Taylor last Tuesday and came to Paris on a combined business and pleasure trip. He will return to Louisville to make his future home.

During his visit, Lyons found employment as a bookkeeper with the Paris Gas & Electric Co. and decided to remain in Paris. Perhaps Lyons' decision to stay in Paris was influenced by meeting Nell Marrs, a popular teacher of Household Economics at the Paris High School. Nell hailed from Lawrenceburg, Ky., and, like Lyons, came from a well-respected family. Nell had attended the same school in Harrodsburg, Ky., as Lyons' mother, after it had been renamed Beaumont College by its new president in 1894. Nell was also a graduate of the Thomas Training School of Home Economics in Detroit, Mich. The Bourbon News described her as a cultured and charming young woman.

Nell appeared to be the perfect match for Lyons. When hired at the Paris Gas & Electric Company, Lyons was described as "a young man of excellent habits and good business training, [who] will make a good man in the position."[7] A few months before the couple married, Lyons joined the Big Four Motor Company, a general garage, repair, and vulcanizing business at the corner of 8th and High Streets in Paris. During the 1920 election of new officials at the Motor Company, Lyons was named the secretary and superintendent of the vulcanizing department.

The Bourbon News, Paris, Ky., October 29, 1920

The Bourbon News, Paris, Ky.,
November 8, 1921

KCERPT:

—Mr. and Mrs. Lyons Board, of
Paris, are the happy parents of a
ne daughter, born at the home of
Mrs. Board's parents, in Lawrenceburg, last week. Mrs. Board before
her marriage, was Miss Nell Marr,
a member of the Paris High School
faculty.

Lyons and Nell married in Lawrenceburg in November 1920 and returned to Paris following their hon-
eymoon trip to Louisville and French
Lick Springs. In October of the following year, they became parents of
a beautiful daughter, Mary Marrs
Board.

Happy times came to a standstill
not long after Mary Marrs' birth.
Lyons faced a serious legal matter with embarrassing repercussions.
Without the consent and against the express order of his friend John L.
Childers, Lyons took Mr. Childers' vehicle and wrecked it. The judgment
against him was $1,000.

1922 Oakland 6-44
Six Sedan

Lyons Board was employed with Big Four Motor Co. in Paris, Ky., when he stole his friend's Oakland Sedan, similar to the auto pictured above.

BOURBON CIRCUIT COURT.

JOHN L. CHILDERS,   PLAINTIFF,

    VS.   PETITION.

LYONS BOARD,   DEFENDANT.

####################

    The plaintiff states that on or about the _____ day of October,1921 the plaintiff owned an Oakland Sedan Automobile of the value of One Thousand Dollars ($1000.00) and that the defendant, without the consent of the plaintiff and against his express orders, wrongfully took possession and charge of and converted to his own use and wrongfully started on a journey with said machine and tore it up and destroyed it to plaintiff's damage in the sum of at least $1000.00, no part of which has been paid.

    Wherefore, the plaintiff prays judgment against the defendant for $1000.00 in damages; for costs and all proper relief.

                                       Attorneys for Plaintiff.

Lyons found himself at a life-changing crossroad. Should he deal with the consequences of his actions or simply abandon the life he had created for himself and run? Sometime in late 1921, Lyons left Paris, never to return. His wife and daughter returned to family in Lawrenceburg, never again having knowledge of Lyons' whereabouts.

Similar strands weave amid the lives of William Lyons Board, who at 8 years old had been asked to identify his mother's assailant, and George Thomas Carter, the man who lost his life because of it.

Similarities:

- Both were young men from good families when legal difficulties disrupted their lives.
- Both were charged with serious offenses.
- Both were married with minor dependents.

Differences:

- *Race*: Lyons was white; George, black.
- *Offense*: Lyons—auto theft and damage; George—attempted assault.
- *Judgment*: Lyons—charged with a civil offense; George—no criminal trial conducted for assault charge before defendant was mob lynched for another unspecified charge.
- *Consequence*: Lyons had the freedom to run. George was lynched.

Mary Lake Board faced more heartache. Two of her children had died; the surviving child, Lyons, made a choice that absented him from her life. One has to suppose she grieved her deceased children and her husband as well as her prodigal son. She and Bill had poured all their hopes into their only surviving child. Perhaps the mantle of his distinguished grandfather, Dr. L. D. Barnes, grew to be a burden for him as the only surviving grandchild. Lyons found himself caught between upholding the expectations and social contract expected of him or making his way on his own far removed from his family and its history. Fatefully, he chose the latter, leaving yet another infant girl without a father.

Unshackling oneself of the past brings instantaneous relief, but at what cost? Lyons must have experienced sleepless nights riddled with guilt after abandoning his wife, newborn daughter, adoring mother, and the Parisian community who highly esteemed him. Yet he quickly relinquished a life he perhaps felt he hadn't measured up to.

With that decision, he attempted to leave behind:

- His family's expectations
- A false narrative that the local newspapers had created about his heroism during the Great War
- His role as an 8-year-old boy in having a man lynched
- Payments he couldn't cover relating to the civil lawsuit against him

Lyons' life on the run took him to various states, including Ohio, Florida, South Carolina, Maryland, Washington, and Oregon. After leaving Paris, he primarily found employment as a chef or a cook. Lyons married at least five times, though he never divorced Nell, who outlived him. He was a stepfather to several of his wives' children, but his only biological child was Mary Marrs.

William Lyons Board died in 1946 at age 53 in Oregon. His mother, Mary Lake Board, had predeceased him in 1934, evidently prior to any reconciliation. Her obituary does not mention him.

The Courier-Journal, Louisville, Ky., December 3, 1934

Mrs. Lake Barnes Board.

Mrs. Lake Barnes Board, widow of W. E. Board, formerly a Paris, Ky., banker, died at 5 o'clock Sunday afternoon at the Church Home and Infirmary. Mrs. Board has been in Louisville fourteen years. She is survived by a granddaughter, Miss Mary Morris Board, Lawrenceburg, Ky. Funeral services will be held at 9 o'clock Tuesday morning at Pearson's, 1310 South Third Street. Burial will be in the Paris Cemetery at Paris.

The day after Mrs. Board's death marked 33 years since the attempted purse snatching near the 2nd Street covered bridge.

The Courier-Journal, Louisville,
Ky., November 23, 1947

Engagement photo of Lyons'
daughter, Mary Marrs
Board

Despite an absent father, Lyons' daughter, Mary Marrs Board, graduated from college in 1943. During World War II, she worked as a chemist for Seagram's in Lawrenceburg, Ky., and Lawrenceburg, Ind., and then worked for the Navy in Honolulu. Upon returning to Kentucky after the war, she married John C. Goodlett, a Lawrenceburg native and recent First Lieutenant in Patton's Army, who was pursuing a Ph.D. at Harvard. While in Massachusetts they had two daughters, in 1957 and 1959, and then moved to Baltimore, where Goodlett was a professor in the Department of Geography at Johns Hopkins. He died unexpectedly of a heart attack in 1967.

Mary Marrs, like George Carter's widow, Mary Eliza, was left to raise two young daughters alone. Like her mother, Nell—after being abandoned by Lyons—Mary Marrs returned to Lawrenceburg, seeking the comfort of family. But only Nell's sister remained. Nell had died in 1952.[8]

Chapter 18

OBSERVATIONS

Let's be clear: George Carter was never charged with a capital crime that should have resulted in the loss of his life. Furthermore, the crime reported in the local newspaper that was allegedly committed against Mrs. W. E. Board was an attempted purse snatching. If the mob lynched Carter for the crime against Mrs. Board, the question remaining is: Was he even the man on that bridge with her that chilly December evening?

In the absence of a fair trial with witnesses and all the other information that has been lost through time, determining the answer to that question is difficult. However, by carefully scrutinizing the circumstances of the incident and the associated news reporting, one can certainly make a claim for Carter's innocence. No one, however, can argue that the entire incident was not an egregious miscarriage of justice.

Following are some important points to consider:

- THE ATTACKER'S PHYSICAL DESCRIPTION
  The crime occurred on December 3, 1900, and Lake Board evidently provided a description of her assailant that was published in the December 5 edition of The Kentuckian-Citizen: the assailant was a burly negro man with brown skin and weight of about 200 pounds. From the available photo evidence, we can ascertain that George Carter was neither burly nor anywhere near 200 pounds. He had a slim build. Interestingly, the description of Mrs. Board's attacker printed in the newspaper matches exactly the description of

the negro attacker of Mrs. Peter Crow in Paris in 1889. Was this merely a stereotype used in many of these reports? Was it accurate?

- POOR VISIBILITY AT THE TIME OF THE ATTACK
The alleged assault occurred about 6 p.m., after the sun had set at 5:17 p.m. on that December day. The area near and inside the covered bridge would have been dark and obscured, making it a good place to commit a crime. Visibility would have been poor, and it would have been difficult for the victim to have gotten a good look at her assailant. Newspapers stated that Mrs. Board recognized her assailant in the "dim light" or "semi-darkness," but the chances of mistaken identity would have been magnified. That means both her initial description of the man may have been flawed, and/or her identification of the man presented in the photo could be questioned. Nevertheless, both Mrs. Board and her 8-year-old son positively identified George Carter as her assailant.

- EXAGGERATED DESCRIPTION AND DEFAMATION OF CHARACTER
The Bourbon News' physical description of George Carter before the lynching was intended to incite fear and racial bias and does not match the available photographs of George Carter: "Carter has a villainous, lecherous face, with protruding eye balls and unusually thick lips."[1] The newspaper also implied that George's crime was something wholly different than a purse snatching, calling one who commits such crimes on the female community an "inhuman brute."[2] The paper then made a case for mob justice, stating that in these situations "there is some excuse for them taking the law into their own hands, and dealing out to them what they would eventually get in the end."[3]

Furthermore, George's criminal history was exaggerated. Currently available records only confirm one period of detention in the state penitentiary. The other criminal charges reported in the newspaper—such as serving time in

the penitentiary a second time for stealing lard, belonging
to a gang of thieves that terrorized Paris, and having been
charged with sexual assault three additional times—could
not be corroborated. No documentation has been found to
support these claims.

By defaming his character and ridiculing his physical appearance, the newspapers dehumanized Carter and attempted to
justify any punishment meted out to him, whether just or
unjust.

- ### Presumption of guilt
  At the time of George Carter's arrest, there was no evidence
  that he was Lake Board's assailant. Before she and her son,
  Lyons, identified him, The Bourbon News stated, "Should
  she do so it might be possible that the many friends of herself
  and husband might make an attempt to take the law into
  their own hands."[4] Through biased news reporting, George
  was presumed the assailant before being identified by Mary
  Lake Board and her son.

- ### Distorted understanding of the crime committed
  The initial report of the crime clearly states that it was a
  robbery attempt. A burly negro man attempted to grab Mrs.
  Board's pocketbook. On the 70th day following the crime,
  George Carter was lynched. During those 70 days, the
  nature of the crime against Mary Lake Board morphed from
  attempted robbery into attempted rape.

- ### Scapegoat justice
  Paris' police department was feeling the pressure to find
  Mrs. Board's assailant. "Constant efforts were made by the
  police to detect the negro, but without avail until last week,
  when Bessie Smoot of Ruckerville, caused a warrant to be
  issued for George Carter, her brother-in-law, on a charge
  of assault," reported the Buffalo Evening News.[5] After his
  arrest, George became the police department's scapegoat.
  Based on the timing of his arrest, his race, and his criminal

background, the newspaper used inflammatory rhetoric to convince the community that George Carter was indeed Mrs. Board's assaulter. The reporter and the editor served as the jury. The mob executed its idea of just punishment.

- **BIASED NEWS REPORTING**
  Reporting by local and national news organizations across America was slanted negatively against George Carter. Each publication was complicit in the lynching by pre-judging Carter's character and by manipulating facts to incite a cry for vengeance. Their inflammatory words made the mob justice more palatable and justifiable. For white America, justice could not wait.

Chapter 19

A PROVIDENTIAL ENCOUNTER

My interest in this story began around 2013 when my mother gave me a Paris Daily Enterprise news clipping entitled "A skeleton in Bourbon's closet," dated September 29, 1978. After getting over the initial shock that a lynching was part of my hometown's history, I leaned on my genealogy research skills and began reviewing newspapers from the 1900–01 period. My friend Lindrell Blackwell and I exchanged information and discussed the results of our research. Shortly afterward, life became busy, so I put the story aside but kept it in the deep recesses of my heart.

In February 2020 I returned to Paris for my mother's funeral. During my extended stay, I worked on ancestry research at the Paris-Bourbon County Public Library and the Bourbon County Courthouse. I was eager to hear about Lindrell's efforts to organize the cleanup of Cedar Heights, a historical African American cemetery in Paris. During this time, Lindrell encouraged me to write about the lynching of George Carter. He later texted me the contact information for a Carter descendant, James (Jim) Bannister.

After returning to my Texas home, I decided to give a courtesy call to Mr. Bannister, the grandson of George Carter's sister Katie. Deep inside I was resigned to abandoning the story due to its emotional impact, but after speaking with Jim, the fire that once burned inside was rekindled. Jim was eager to learn more, and with my love of research, I knew I could fill in some of the blanks for him and his family. I immediately picked up the research where I had left off some six years earlier. I scanned online newspapers, tracked ancestors through Ancestry.com, and Googled information about the incident.

Two weeks into my research, I Googled "George Carter Paris KY 1901." Several pages of results appeared but one stood out: a Murky Press blog that included an entry titled "Time Stands Still" dated 11/30/2019. Its author stated that her grandfather "spent a lifetime coming to grips with the perverted justice he witnessed as an eight-year-old boy in Paris, Ky."[1] My interest was piqued, and I reached out to the author for any information that her grandfather may have shared.

On June 17, 2020, I received this email reply from the author:

> *"Thank you for reaching out to me. I'm afraid all the information I have about George Carter comes from newspaper accounts. A friend of mine was doing some genealogical research for me and, upon searching for information about my great-grandmother Mary Lake Barnes Board, initially stumbled across a story about the lynching in a California newspaper. I doubt I have to describe my horror in learning that my ancestors had in any way been associated with a man losing his life in this way. My great-grandmother died in 1934, and my grandfather William Lyons Board—who witnessed the "assault" at age 8—died in 1946. He had left Paris in 1921 or early 1922, shortly after my mother was born, and no one in her family had any further contact with him. So I have no first-hand accounts of how this incident was addressed in my family. As you mentioned in your initial contact with me, my guess is that nobody ever talked about it again."*

After reading her reply, my head was spinning and I had to tell myself, "Breathe!" Do you mean to tell me I'm communicating with the great-granddaughter of Mary Lake Barnes Board, the lady who identified George Carter as her assaulter? I was in the middle of researching the author's family! What are the odds of this encounter happening? Surely this was a providential opportunity. As I sat trying to wrap my brain around the significance of this exchange, my only response to Sallie Showalter was, "May I now call you on your cell?"

Since that time, we have exchanged numerous emails and enjoyed numerous telephone conversations. Getting to know Sallie has been a joy. She is a kind, fearless, and generous spirit with a sense of fairness that is obvious through her gift of writing. She mailed me a copy of her latest book, *Next Train Out*, about her grandfather, William Lyons Board. Although the book is a work of fiction, it carefully follows the details of his life and was a tremendous help in filling in some of the blanks about her family. Sallie also volunteered to assist with research, contacting the Kentucky Department for Libraries & Archives in Frankfort, Ky., for information about George Carter.

These encounters with both Jim and Sallie have been gifts to me. Both individuals are towers of strength and intelligent and compassionate human beings...evidencing strong family stock. Through discussions with them, it became apparent that the two were interested in meeting one another to discuss their ancestors and their link to the 1901 lynching. When I suggested a meeting, both responded positively. The door was now open for a present-day engagement between the two families connected to a 120-year-old incident in Bourbon County, Ky. I hoped the meeting would help both parties initiate the healing they needed and that a friendship might grow between them.

Chapter 20

THE DESCENDANTS MEET

Sallie Showalter and Jim Bannister, July 15, 2020. [Photos courtesy of Bobby Shiflet Images]

More than a century has passed since that cold night in February 1901. Through all that time, our ancestors spoke little about what happened.

On Wednesday, July 15, 2020, the tentacles of whispered secrets breached the consciousness of two descendants of the accused and the accuser. The two families came together in the basement of Paris' Hopewell Museum to discuss that horrid night and its impact on both families. Jim Bannister, great-nephew of George Carter, and Sallie Showalter, great-granddaughter of Mary Lake Board, met for the first time. In the words of moderator Lindrell Blackwell, Jim and Sallie took the first steps to bring the skeleton out of Bourbon County's closet.

To ensure social distancing amidst the COVID-19 pandemic, Jim and Sallie sat at opposite ends of an oblong table with Lindrell nearby. Tom Martin's team from radio station 88.9 WEKU recorded the entire conversation.[1] Brief excerpts from that conversation follow.

Sallie began the discussion, "The first thing I want to say is how sorry I am that my family had anything to do with a loss of your family member for absolutely no reason whatsoever." It had been about six years since she had learned that her family had been involved in the incident in 1901. As she told the story, one evening about 7 o'clock while working at Transylvania University, her next-door neighbor Charles Camp, a retired investigative reporter, sent her an email. He had been helping Sallie find information about her grandfather Williams Lyons Board, who had completely disappeared from her family's life in 1921. Camp had stumbled across a newspaper article in a California paper about George Carter being accused of having assaulted Sallie's great-grandmother and eventually being lynched for that crime.

Sallie stated that she hadn't been the same since. "Hopefully things that happened 120 years ago will be brought to light so that people in Paris and people across Kentucky can understand that these things happen. We can put our heads in the sand and pretend like these things never happened, but they happen in families that you least expected."

Born in 1940, Jim has lived in Paris most of his life. He attended Paris Western High School, the town's colored school. He explained how black people were intimidated into not mentioning what had gone on before. Jim asked older people in Paris about the 1901 lynching but couldn't get any information.

Jim has wonderful memories of his grandmother, Katie Carter Spencer Lee, who raised him along with his mother. Katie was only 7 years old when her brother George Thomas Carter was lynched. Until she was laid to rest in 1985, her brother's murder weighed heavy on her heart. Seldom did she speak of this horrific incident that had profoundly affected her life. When she did talk about it, she softly uttered painful words with her head bowed. It was as though the weight of her words was too heavy to bear.

Katie would let out a little bit of information at a time, but Jim could never get many details. When he was about 10 years old, his grandmother told him, "Sit down. I have something to explain to you." Once he sat down, the words poured from her lips, "They lynched my brother." As a young lad, Jim didn't fully comprehend the meaning of her words but waited patiently as his grandmother continued her story.

Katie's account of what happened vastly differs from the 1901 newspaper accounts. She stated that there was a feed store on Pleasant Street where George went one morning to purchase chicken feed. He noticed a lady a few feet behind him, whom he acknowledged by respectfully bowing his head and tipping his hat. According to Jim's grandmother, that fateful encounter led to the lynching of her brother. Katie said that her brother was murdered on the railroad trestle that runs along Pleasant Street. Members of the mob then carried his body from the railroad trestle to the gate in front of the courthouse where his body was displayed all day. Many people gathered to view the body, but nothing was ever done, and little was spoken about it.

Since that tender age, Jim had hidden the few words his grandmother shared deep in his heart. He yearned to know more about what happened to his great-uncle George.

"It was just devastating, really, but I'm getting to understand what it's all about now and that helped me out so much," said Jim. He thanked Sallie for coming forward with her story. "By you coming forward with that I think that's the most wonderful thing that you can contribute to what's going on today, because we don't have people to come together and talk. That's what we need."

Jim has three children, five grandchildren, and two great-grandchildren. "It's so important because they need to know everything that has happened so that they can do something about it." Marvin Gaye has a song called "What's Going On" that's 50 years old and the lyrics are still relevant today, says Jim.

Sallie hopes the community in Paris can have an honest conversation about this history and, in some way, recognize formally that Jim's great-uncle lost his life due to an unjust act. It's also important for the community to note that another gentleman lost his life in a similar incident in 1889. There may be others as well. Only by recognizing the past can we address the underlying problems.

View from 8th Street of the Paris Post Office, located at 800 Pleasant Street. [Photo courtesy of the Hopewell Museum]

The Hopewell Museum, formerly the Paris Post Office and the site of the meeting between the two descendants in July 2020. [Google photo captured June 2019]

Chapter 21

CONCLUSION

There's nothing more important at this moment than heeding the lessons gleaned from our history. One critical lesson is understanding that justice does not lie in man's desire for avenging a wrong with self-satisfying motives. It is every person's constitutional right to be awarded blind justice, i.e., justice that is blind to power, race, wealth, or position.

In the foregoing pages we have reviewed a heinous crime, the lynching of George Thomas Carter, a 21-year old African American citizen of Paris, Ky. He was a son, brother, husband, and father. By all accounts, George was not perfect and some decisions he made brought serious consequences, but does imperfection warrant no justice? Truth rings in Maceo Bishop's assessment, "They just wanted a negro to hang during those times." For clearly it was the mob's intent to lynch a black man. For them, the legal process was too slow. Punishment for assaulting a white woman had to be meted swift and sure. Unfortunately, getting to the truth was never the goal.

George didn't stand a chance. Upon his arrest for the alleged crime against his sister-in-law, the assault on his character began. Reports exaggerated his criminal history, ridiculed his facial features, and distorted the alleged crime to justify the lynching. By dehumanizing him, the printed words molded George into the perfect villain and concluded that he was undeserving of justice and of life.

Today we ponder why America is still grappling with racial disparities in our justice system. J. R. Taylor well states our dilemma, "A history of tolerance for violence has laid the groundwork for injustice today."[1]

There's been some slow progress toward tearing down the barriers of discrimination, yet cries for justice still ripple through communities of color. When the lens of your heart is shaded with hatred, you're incapable of viewing others as your equal. Common decency is impaired. How does a racist purge a mindset that is deeply rooted in malevolent influences and develop a moral compass that guides the heart?

Self-examination is essential. The ills of our society will continue to proliferate unless each person embarks on an inward journey. We must examine our thoughts and our intent toward others, particularly others unlike ourselves. Our history should be the yardstick by which we measure our progress as a society. Unless we heed the mistakes of times past, these atrocious crimes against our fellow man will recur. As Sallie Showalter eloquently pens, "Burying [the past] will only let the cancer grow. Bringing it into the light…is how we may best be able to change course."[2]

Jim wisely stated, "Try to understand what each individual is all about. We need to discuss and laugh about it because it's already happened, and we don't want to see it happen again." Thus, communication is critical. Open and honest dialogues about race among people of different backgrounds are necessary to heal and to build a bridge of trust and respect.

Reaching back through history on eagle's wings can help us learn from mistakes made by our ancestors in Bourbon County in February 1901. This is important in building a better world today as well as for future generations. History, whether good or bad, is always in our rearview mirror. History can never be obliterated. It forever remains within us, either consciously or subconsciously, and lays bare our mistakes for all humanity to acknowledge. We must use these opportunities to reflect, educate, forgive, heal, and move forward as better human beings.

The late Justice Ruth Bader Ginsburg best encapsulates the significance of our memories guiding us: "In striving to drain dry the waters of prejudice and oppression, we must rely on measures of our own creation—upon the wisdom of our laws and the decency of our institutions, upon our reasoning minds and our feeling hearts. And as a constant spark to carry on, upon our vivid memories of the evils we wish to banish from our world. In our long struggle for a more just world, our memories are among our most powerful resources."[3]

George Thomas Carter's young life met a horrific end. Let the lessons gleaned from that heinous crime illuminate our understanding and lead us to peace, love, and equality for all people.

NOTES

INTRODUCTION

1. "Interview with Charles Maceo Bishop, November 5, 1988," Louie B. Nunn Center for Oral History, University of Kentucky Libraries, Project: Blacks in Lexington Oral History Project, https://kentuckyoralhistory.org/ark:/16417/xt7dv40jwn9q.

2. George C. Wright, *Racial Violence in Kentucky, 1865-1940 – Lynchings, Mob Rule, and "Legal Lynchings"* (Baton Rouge: Louisiana State University Press, 1996), 59-60.

3. George C. Wright, *A History of Blacks in Kentucky: In Pursuit of Equality, 1890-1980*, vol. 2 (Frankfort, Ky.: Kentucky Historical Society, 1992), 79.

4. Ibid., 81-82.

5. Karl Raitz and Nancy O'Malley, *Kentucky's Frontier Highway – Historical Landscapes along the Maysville Road* (Lexington, Ky.: The University Press of Kentucky, 2012), 171.

6. "Interview with Charles Maceo Bishop," https://kentuckyoralhistory.org/ark:/16417/xt7dv40jwn9q.

7. Wright, *A History of Blacks in Kentucky*, 86.

8. Ibid., 78.

9. Ibid., 84.

10. "Confronting Decades of Inaction, Senate Unanimously Approves Anti-Lynching Bill," Equal Justice Initiative, January 7, 2019, https://eji.org/news/senate-unanimously-approves-anti-lynching-bill/.

11. Stanford *Semi-Weekly Interior Journal*, July 30, 1889.

Chapter 1: **THE ACCUSED**

1. H. E. Everman, *Bourbon County Since 1865 (H. E. Everman, 1999)*, 37.

2. *Claysville and Ruckerville: Historically Black Neighborhoods in Paris, Kentucky*, Hopewell Museum, Exhibit, Paris, Ky.

3. Houston Hartsfield Holloway, *In His Own Words: Houston Hartsfield Holloway's Slavery, Emancipation, and Ministry in Georgia*, ed. David E. Paterson (Macon, Ga.: Mercer University Press, 2015), 134.

4. *Claysville and Ruckerville*, Hopewell Museum, Exhibit, Paris, Ky.

5. Wright, *A History of Blacks in Kentucky*, 118.

6. "Paris and Bourbon Sketched," *The Bourbon News*, January 28, 1898.

7. Everman, *Bourbon County Since 1865*, 53.

8. "Commonwealth of Ky. vs. George Carter—Minutes of trial," Kentucky Department for Libraries and Archives, filed June 10, 1899.

Chapter 2: **THE ACCUSER**

1. Beaumont Inn, "History of Beaumont Inn," https://beaumontinn.com/history-of-beaumont-inn/.

2. "Deaths," *The Bourbon News*, [William E. Board's obituary], February 5, 1918.

3. "Personal Mention," Danville *Weekly Advocate*, December 3, 1886.

4. "History of Paris and Bourbon County—Deposit Bank," *The Bourbon News*, October 3, 1905.

Chapter 3: **1900-01 NEWSPAPER SOURCES**

1. Everman, *Bourbon County Since 1865*, 94.
2. Wright, *A History of Blacks in Kentucky*, 47.
3. James Wright, "Whether Lawrenceburg or Kenosha, media should not normalize hate groups and vigilantes," *Lexington Herald-Leader*, September 10, 2020, https://www.kentucky.com/article245377300.html.
4. Ibid.

Chapter 4: **A CLIMATE OF OPPRESSION**

1. "Conspiracy to Oppress and Injure the Negroes— The Charge Against Bourbon Men Brought Before Commissioner Hill; Trick Crap Games Alleged," *The Morning Herald*, November 2, 1900.
2. G. C. Wright, *A History of Blacks in Kentucky*, 94.
3. Ibid., 96.
4. Brian Lyman, "Fact check: Yes, historians do teach that first Black members of Congress were Republicans," *USA Today*, June 20, 2020, https://www.usatoday.com/story/news/factcheck/2020/06/18/fact-check-democrats-republicans-and-complicated-history-race/3208378001/.
5. G. C. Wright, *A History of Blacks in Kentucky*, 93.
6. Ibid.

Chapter 5: **THE ROBBERY ATTEMPT**

1. "Silently and Surely—Not a Sound Uttered by Lynchers as They Did Their Work—Iglored [sic] Culprit Swung in the Air—Warning to Negroes Who Assault White Woman—Panic Among Colored Prisoners In the Jail Where Mob's victim Was Imprisoned," *The Evening Bulletin*, February 12, 1901.
2. "Bad Man—Hanged At Courthouse Gate At Paris.— George Carter the Victim.—Mob Composed of About Twenty-five Men. —The Negro's Black Record," Louisville *Courier-Journal*, February 12, 1901.

Chapter 6: **THE MANHUNT AND AN ARREST**

1. "Bad Man," Louisville *Courier-Journal*, February 12, 1901.

Chapter 7: **THE EXAMINING TRIAL**

1. "Held for Attempted Assault," *The Bourbon News*, February 8, 1901.
2. Ibid.
3. Ibid.
4. "Judge Lynch—Wreaks Sure and Swift Vengeance on Geo. Carter, the Assaulter of Mrs. Board.—Quiet and Orderly, But Determined," *The Bourbon News*, February 12, 1901.
5. Ibid.

Chapter 8: **THE IDENTIFICATION**

1. "Judge Lynch," *The Bourbon News*, February 12, 1901.
2. "Bad Man," Louisville *Courier-Journal*, February 12, 1901.
3. "Body Found Hanging at Dawn," *The Morning Herald*, February 12, 1901.
4. Jennifer R. Taylor, "A History of Tolerance for Violence Has Laid the Groundwork for Injustice Today," American Bar Association, May 16, 2019, https://www.americanbar.org/groups/crsj/publications/human_rights_magazine_home/black-to-the-future/tolerance-for-violence/.
5. "Murdered in Ruckerville," *The Bourbon News*, April 11, 1899.
6. "Judge Lynch," *The Bourbon News*, February 12, 1901.

Chapter 9: **FEBRUARY 11, 1901**

1. "Body Found Hanging at Dawn," *The Morning Herald*, February 12, 1901.
2. "Judge Lynch," *The Bourbon News*, February 12, 1901.
3. Ibid.

4. Jailer Allen Kiser's official affidavit regarding the lynching of George Carter, Kentucky Department for Libraries and Archives, February 1901.

5. "Silently and Surely," *The Evening Bulletin*, February 12, 1901.

6. "Judge Lynch," *The Bourbon News*, February 12, 1901.

7. Ibid.

8. Ibid.

9. *The Evening Bulletin*, February 13, 1901.

10. "Judge Lynch Again—This Time It Is In Kentucky. George Carter, a Negro, Who Assaulted Mrs. W. E. Board," Stockton *Daily Evening Record*, February 11, 1901.

11. "Body Found Hanging at Dawn," *The Morning Herald*, February 12, 1901.

12. "Judge Lynch," *The Bourbon News*, February 12, 1901.

13. Ibid.

14. "The President on Lynching. Gov. Durbin Commended for the Attitude Resumed Recently," *The Bourbon News*, August 11, 1903.

Chapter 10: ATTEMPTED ROBBERY VS. RAPE

1. "Kentucky Mob Lynches A Negro Accused of Assaulting a Woman," *The San Francisco Call*, February 12, 1901.

2. *Mount Vernon Signal*, February 15, 1901.

3. Chloe Angyal, "I Don't Want to Be an Excuse for Racist Violence Anymore—White women's passive role in racist attacks like Charleston," The New Republic, June 22, 2015, https://newrepublic.com/article/122110/i-dont-want-be-excuse-racist-violence-charleston.

4. Jessie Daniels, "White Women and the Defense of Lynching," *Racism Review*, February 11, 2014, http://www.racismreview.com/blog/2014/02/11/white-women-defense-lynching/.

Chapter 11: **DÉJÀ VU**

1. "Justice!—Jim Kelly, a Paris Rapist, Lynched by a Furious Mob —For Outrage on the Person of Mrs. Peter Crow, at Her Home. —After a Desperate but Unavailing Three Hours' Struggle," *The Kentucky Leader*, July 26, 1889.
2. "Bourbon Vengeance.—A Negro Brute Left Dangling From a Bridge By Outraged Citizens.—Jim Kelly, the Rape Fiend, Taken From the Jailer At Paris and Dropped Into Eternity," Louisville *Weekly Courier-Journal*, July 29, 1889.
3. Ibid.
4. Ibid.
5. Ibid.
6. "Justice!" *The Kentucky Leader*, July 26, 1889.

Chapter 12: **A REWARD FOR APPREHENSION OF LYNCHERS**

1. "Small Concern With a Big Name.—The International Council of The World Offers a Reward For Apprehension of Lynchers," *The Bourbon News*, February 19, 1901.
2. Christopher M. Clarke, *Samuel Burdett: Black Soldier, Veterinarian, and Civil Rights Activist* (Christopher M. Clarke, July 25, 2017), 7-8.
3. "Small Concern With a Big Name," *The Bourbon News*, February 19, 1901.

Chapter 13: **THE IRONY**

1. G. C. Wright, *A History of Blacks in Kentucky*, 43.

Chapter 14: **OMINOUS WORDS**

1. "Judge Lynch," *The Bourbon News*, February 12, 1901.
2. G. C. Wright, *Racial Violence in Kentucky*, 63.
3. "Judge Lynch," *The Bourbon News*, February 12, 1901.

Chapter 15 **THE BOURBON COURTHOUSE**

1. "Interview with Charles Maceo Bishop," https://kentuckyoralhistory.org/ark:/16417/xt7dv40jwn9q.

2. "Bourbon County Courthouse is Destroyed by Flames," Louisville *Courier-Journal*, October 20, 1901.

Chapter 16: **ANTILYNCHING LEGISLATION**

1. "Bullets Greet A Paris Mob At The Jail—Attempt to Lynch Negro Is Resisted By Jailer Jos. Farris—Eugene Houston Killed Instantly —Alleged Negro Assailant of White Woman Badly Injured," *The Bourbon News*, September 1, 1914.

2. "Negro Taken from Paris Officer is Lynched," *The Bourbon News*, April 2, 1920.

3. "Legislature Passes Mob Suppression Measure," *The Bourbon News*, February 10, 1920.

4. "Negro Taken from Paris Officer is Lynched," *The Bourbon News*, April 2, 1920.

5. John D. Wright Jr., "Lexington's Suppression of the 1920 Will Lockett Lynch Mob," *The Register of the Kentucky Historical Society* 84, no. 3 (1986): 263-79. Accessed March 26, 2021. http://www.jstor.org/stable/23381084.

Chapter 17: **THE AFTERMATH**

1. Deborah Gray White, *Ar'n't I a Woman? Female Slaves in the Plantation South* (New York: W. W. Norton & Company, 1985), 189.

2. G. C. Wright, *A History of Blacks in Kentucky*, 26.

3. Sallie Showalter, *Next Train Out* (Georgetown, Ky.,: Murky Press, 2020), 72.

4. "Personal Mention," *The Bourbon News*, February 18, 1913.

5. Certificate of Death for William Ellery Board, Bureau of Vital Statistics, Commonwealth of Kentucky, 1918.

6. Showalter, *Next Train Out*, 23.

7. "To Take Position with Gas & Electric Co.," *The Bourbon News*, May 27, 1919.

8. Showalter, Biographical sketch of her mother, Mary Marrs Board.

Chapter 18: OBSERVATIONS

1. "Held For Attempted Assault," *The Bourbon News*, February 8, 1901.

2. "Judge Lynch," *The Bourbon News*, February 12, 1901.

3. Ibid.

4. "Held For Attempted Assault," *The Bourbon News*, February 8, 1901.

5. "Kentucky Mob Hangs a Negro.—George Carter, Alleged Assailant of a White Woman, Taken From Jail at Paris and Lynched," *Buffalo Evening News*, February 11, 1901.

Chapter 19: A PROVIDENTIAL ENCOUNTER

1. Showalter, "Time Stands Still," Murky Press blog *Clearing the Fog*, November 30, 2019, https://www.murkypress.com/blog/time-stands-still.

Chapter 20: The Descendants Meet

1. "The Conversation," Eastern Standard, 88.9 WEKU, July 30, 2020, https://esweku.org/track/2431045/the-conversation. For a brief summary of the conversation and Tom Martin's interview with Sallie Showalter for the Eastern Standard program, go to https://esweku.org/track/2429538/tom-martin-with-jim-bannister-sallie-showalter.

Chapter 21: CONCLUSION

1. Taylor, "A History of Tolerance for Violence Has Laid the Groundwork for Injustice Today," American Bar Association, May 16, 2019, https://www.americanbar.org/groups/crsj/publications/human_rights_magazine_home/black-to-the-future/tolerance-for-violence/.

2. Showalter, "Time Stands Still," November 30, 2019, https://www.murkypress.com/blog/time-stands-still.

3. U.S. Supreme Court Justice Ruth Bader Ginsburg, "Jewish Food Hero," https://jewishfoodhero.com/57-quotes-on-ruth-bader-ginsburg-to-guide-us-forward/.

ACKNOWLEDGMENTS

Special thanks to Sallie Showalter for her tireless enthusiasm, generosity, and editorial skills, which helped bring this 1901 story out of the shadows of Bourbon County's history. She graciously shared her book, *Next Train Out*, which provided invaluable information about her ancestors, prominent characters of this story. A path paved with revelations, healing, and friendship began for Sallie, Jim Bannister, and me at destiny's crossroads.

A TRIBUTE TO SALLIE & JIM

Oh how history unfolded can pierce a loving heart
When an old family secret tears your soul apart!
Fearlessly I traveled a path to brighten a life grown dim.
Oh what healing was found for my grateful friend, Jim!

Tessa Bishop Hoggard
8/3/2020

Tessa Bishop Hoggard was born and raised in Paris, Ky., and graduated with a bachelor's degree from Morehead State University in Morehead, Ky. She is now a resident of Dallas County, Texas.